HARRIET TUBMAN
The Moses of Her People

HARRIET TUBMAN
The Moses of Her People

SARAH H. BRADFORD

Introduction by
Butler A. Jones

DOVER PUBLICATIONS, INC.
Mineola, New York

Bibliographical Note

This Dover edition, first published in 2004, is an unabridged republication of the text of the 2nd edition, originally printed by G. R. Lockwood & Son, New York, 1886. The introduction is taken from the edition published by Corinth Books, 1961. The frontispiece is taken from the first edition, published as *Scenes in the Life of Harriet Tubman* by W. J. Moses, Auburn, N.Y., 1869.

International Standard Book Number

ISBN-13: 978-0-486-43858-0
ISBN-10: 0-486-43858-9

Manufactured in the United States by LSC Communications
43858915   2020
www.doverpublications.com

INTRODUCTION

Go down Moses! Way down in Egyptland!
Tell ol' Pharaoh let my people go!

In such simple but dramatic language as this did the slaves of
the plantation South adapt the Jewish story as told in Exodus to
their own situation. For behind this seemingly naive appeal for
a Mosaic emissary to the slave owners lay the slaves' firm belief
that the slave masters' refusal to heed the repeated urgings to
"let my people go" would eventually result in Divine deliverance. Had it not been thus with the children of Israel who, like
the slaves, had been put to labor in a foreign land? Could He do
less for these His children also? There were many who in the
years prior to 1860 undertook the Mosaic mission and appealed
to the plantation owners to abandon the system of chattel slavery.
There were those too who, tiring of the apparent fruitlessness of
these diplomatic missions, took up the mantle of deliverer.
Some of these were notably unsuccessful (Nat Turner and John
Brown, for example) while others, relying upon more devious
means, were notably successful. Among these latter none was
more daring or individually successful than was Harriet
Tubman—the subject of this wholly sympathetic but revealing
biography by Sarah Bradford.

This is an important book. Whatever its shortcomings as an
exercise in classical biography, the story told here is an integral
part of the events which a century ago led to the great American
excursion into fratricide. Those who would dismiss the book on
critical grounds should bear in mind the fact that Harriet
Tubman was not only an illiterate, highly visible run-away slave
but that she was engaged in an illegal activity. Under the circumstances, it should come as no surprise to discover that those who
gave her aid and comfort were not disposed to record that fact
in diary, memoir, or letter—traditional sources of biographical

data. Such documentary evidence would have been fatal to their defense if ever they were brought to trial for aiding a fugitive slave to escape.

The book is not without documentation, however. In this second edition Mrs. Bradford was prescient enough to include in text and appendix letters from, among others, such noted anti-slavery leaders as Gerrit Smith and Thomas Garret. These directly corroborate Harriet's version of the exploits recorded here and lend support to the accuracy of her reports of other journeys into "Egypt-land."

While the subtitle of Mrs. Bradford's book (THE MOSES OF HER PEOPLE) is perhaps a more apt description of Harriet's role in leading more than three hundred of her kinsmen out of the land of bondage, in the male dominated world of her contemporary admirers she was more commonly pictured as an American Joan of Arc. The similarities between the two are interesting though perhaps not especially revealing. Like Joan, Harriet was born among the dispossessed, denied the rudiments of a formal education, reared in a harsh social environment, early enveloped by a simple albeit compulsive religious faith, and was actively sought by the minions of the law because of the price on her head. Like Joan also she was harbored and supported by many persons willing to risk their all in furtherance of her cause. But unlike Joan whose name and deeds have since become a part of the formal learning experience of every Frenchman, neither Harriet's name nor her deeds are an integral part of the education of American youth.

This is not the place for detailed examination of the reasons for this suppression through historical omission. But it is pertinent to remark that in the revisionist theory of the origins of the American Civil War, economic and political forces are emphasized, and humanitarianism is accorded little causal significance. Consequently, those among the abolitionist leaders who cannot be categorized as self-seeking politicians or unrestrained fanatics are frequently omitted from the histories of the period. Yet there can be no real understanding or appreciation of the great drama played out on American soil a century ago without some recognition of the humanitarian "instincts" which motivated some of its principals. Harriet Tubman was exemplar *par excellence* of that humanitarian spirit. What better evidence of this does one need than the absence of bitterness over the government's persistent refusal to reward her for four years of service as occasional agent behind enemy lines, as scout for Union troops in the unfamiliar swamplands of the South, and as practical nurse in Union camp hospitals ministering to all—alike Yankee soldier, captured rebel, and fleeing slave. Through her we are re-introduced to many of those who like her were humanely inspired with no thought of earthly reward to work for the overthrow of slavery. Again we are made aware of the penalties paid by some and the risks assumed by all.

Though Harriet's birthdate is given as 1820 (or 1821) two events occurring in 1793 mark the real beginnings of her story. These were the perfection of the cotton gin and the passage of the Fugitive Slave Law. The former vastly increased the wealth potential of cotton farming and in so doing increased the market value of slaves. The latter established the legal right of recovery of run-away slaves wherever found in the United States. By provision of this law a slave owner or his agent could arrest an alleged fugitive, haul him before a local magistrate, and if able to convince that person of the validity of his claim, return with the "run-away" to his home. In practical terms this meant that every Negro, freeman or fugitive, ran the risk of being impressed into slavery by the simple expedient of having some white man appear and assert a claim of ownership. The risk loses its remoteness when it is remembered that descriptions of run-away slaves tended to be vague and general. Any Negro bearing a passing resemblance to the alleged fugitive and unable immediately to produce documentary proof of his "free status" was likely to be surrendered to the claimant white. Mrs. Bradford has graphically described Harriet's determined and successful effort to rescue one such victim of this procedure. There were several other such incidents (not all reported here) in the life of this forceful antagonist of slavery.

While the records of the day do not permit us to say with certainty whether or not many free Negroes were impressed into slavery by these means, the vigor with which run-aways were sought, the alacrity with which some magistrates acceded to the requests of slave owners, plus the contemporary news reports of certain magisterial hearings lead us to believe that the number was not insignificant. In an effort to reduce the number of such instances to a minimum and also as a means of forestalling the return of actual run-aways many of the Free States enacted Personal Liberty Laws. These generally required a more elaborate hearing as to the facts of the case (in some states a jury determination was required) before an alleged fugitive might be returned to his so-called owner. But it was the threat to the free Negro together with the shocking scenes of recovered run-aways being marched through the streets of northern towns that made abolitionists like Sarah Bradford refer to the period prior to 1860 as "the years of terror of the Fugitive Slave Law."

For such leaders of the anti-slavery movement as Harriet Tubman, the Personal Liberty Laws were never more than instruments of convenience to be used to delay and occasionally prevent the return of run-aways. Ultimate success for their program of subverting slavery by promoting effective escape required (1) a guaranteed haven for those who succeeded in escaping and (2) a reasonably safe escape route by which the fugitive could come to the place of safety. Once it became evident that our neighbor to the north would provide the haven, the terminus of the escape route was fixed and the underground railroad was born. But the path from plantation slave cabins to Canada was a circuitous one requiring many stop-overs. With only the North Star to guide them, escaping slaves might easily be apprehended by their owner-pursuers or fall prey to the wiles of professional slave chasers. What was needed were men and women familiar with the ways of the chase who were prepared to journey into the Southland, organize small bands of escapees and escort them from one stop-over point (called junctions) to the other in the long trek from plantation to Canada. Dubbed "conductors" these intrepid persons became the real heroes and heroines of the Underground Railroad. And of the many who served in this capacity none was more resourceful, more elusive, more eagerly hunted (rewards for her capture at one time totalled $40,000), or more successful than Harriet Tubman.

Mrs. Bradford does not tell us much about Harriet's life after her return to her home in Auburn (New York) following the close of the Civil War. But that too is a fascinating tale. This illiterate and penniless woman, now aged far beyond her years and suffering from frequent and prolonged periods of somnolence, immediately upon her return set about to save her home from mortgage foreclosure, to care for her own now very aged parents, and to urge the establishment of a home for the indigent aged Negroes of the community. When after several years of effort it appeared that insufficient funds would be raised to build such a home for the aged, Harriet cheerfully converted her own quarters to this purpose. Touched by her selflessness the people of Auburn rallied to her aid and established the Harriet Tubman Home for Aged and Indigent Negroes. After her death in 1913 a subscription campaign was launched to collect funds for a monument in the town square. The campaign was soon subscribed and the monument stands today in mute testimony to a woman of indomitable will—truly a Moses of Her People who having led them out of the land of Egypt, out of the House of Bondage and into the land of Canaan now sought to make meaningful the promise of freedom.

Butler A. Jones
Ohio Wesleyan University

HARRIET

The Moses of Her People

BY
SARAH H. BRADFORD

"Farewell, ole Marster, don't think hard of me,
I'm going on to Canada, where all de slaves are free."

"Jesus, Jesus will go wid you,
He will lead you to His throne,
He who died has gone before you,
Trod de wine-press all alone."

PREFACE

THE title I have given my black heroine, in this second edition of her story, viz.: THE MOSES OF HER PEOPLE, may seem a little ambitious, considering that this Moses was a woman, and that she succeeded in piloting only three or four hundred slaves from the land of bondage to the land of freedom.

But I only give her here the name by which she was familiarly known, both at the North and the South, during the years of terror of the Fugitive Slave Law, and during our last Civil War, in both of which she took so prominent a part.

And though the results of her unexampled heroism were not to free a whole nation of bond-men and bond-women, yet this object was as much the desire of her heart, as it was of that of the great leader of Israel. Her cry to the slave-holders, was ever like his to Pharaoh, "Let my people go!" and not even he imperiled life and limb more willingly, than did our courageous and self-sacrificing friend.

Her name deserves to be handed down to posterity, side by side with the names of Jeanne D'Arc, Grace Darling, and Florence Nightingale, for not one of these women, noble and brave as they were, has shown more courage, and power of endurance, in facing danger and death to relieve human suffering, than this poor black woman, whose story I am endeavoring in a most imperfect way to give you.

Would that Mrs. Stowe had carried out the plan she once projected, of being the historian of our sable friend; by her graphic pen, the incidents of such a life might have been wrought up into a tale of thrilling interest, equaling, if not exceeding her world renowned "Uncle Tom's Cabin."

The work fell to humbler hands, and the first edition of this story, under the title of "Harriet Tubman," was written in the greatest possible haste, while the writer was preparing for a voyage to Europe. There was pressing need for this book, to save the poor woman's little home from being sold under a mortgage, and letters and facts were penned down rapidly, as they came in. The book has now been in part re-written and the letters and testimonials placed in an appendix.

For the satisfaction of the incredulous (and there will naturally be many such, when so strange a tale is repeated to them), I will here state that so far as it has been possible, I have received corroboration of every incident related to me by my heroic friend. I did this for the satisfaction of others, not for my own. No one can hear Harriet talk, and not believe every word she says. As Mr. Sanborn says of her, "she is too *real* a person, not to be true."

Many incidents quite as wonderful as those related in the story, I have rejected, because I had no way in finding the persons who could speak to their truth.

This woman was the friend of William H. Seward, of Gerritt Smith, of Wendell Phillips, of William Lloyd Garrison, and of many other distinguished philanthropists before the War, as of very many officers of the Union Army during the conflict.

After her almost superhuman efforts in making her own escape from slavery, and then returning to the South *nineteen times,* and bringing away with her over three hundred fugitives, she was sent by Governor Andrew of Massachusetts to the South at the beginning of the War, to act as spy and scout for our armies, and to be employed as hospital nurse when needed.

Here for four years she labored without any remuneration, and during the time she was acting as nurse, never drew but twenty days' rations from our Government. She managed to support herself, as well as to take care of the suffering soldiers.

Secretary Seward exerted himself in every possible way to procure her a pension from Congress, but red-tape proved too strong even for him, and her case was rejected, because it did not come under any recognized law.

The first edition of this little story was published through the liberality of Gerritt Smith, Wendell Phillips, and prominent men in Auburn, and the object for which it was written was accomplished. But that book has long been out of print, and the facts stated there are all unknown to the present generation.

There have, I am told, often been calls for the book, which could not be answered, and I have been urged by many friends as well as by Harriet herself, to prepare another edition. For another necessity has arisen and she needs help again not for herself, but for certain helpless ones of her people.

Her own sands are nearly run, but she hopes, 'ere she goes home, to see this work, a hospital, well under way. Her last breath and her last efforts will be spent in the cause of those for whom she has already risked so much.

> For them her tears will fall,
> For them her prayers ascend;
> To them her toils and cares be given,
> Till toils and cares shall end.
>   S. H. B.

Letter from Mr. Oliver Johnson for the second edition:

NEW YORK, *March* 6, 1886.

MY DEAR MADAM:

I am very glad to learn that you are about to publish a revised edition of your life of that heroic woman, Harriet Tubman, by whose assistance so many American slaves were enabled to break their bonds.

During the period of my official connection with the Anti-Slavery office in New York, I saw her frequently, when she came there with the companies of slaves, whom she had successfully piloted away from the South; and often listened with wonder to the story of her adventures and hair-breadth escapes.

She always told her tale with a modesty which showed how unconscious she was of having done anything more than her simple duty. No one who listened to her could doubt her perfect truthfulness and integrity.

Her shrewdness in planning the escape of slaves, her skill in avoiding arrest, her courage in every emergency, and her willingness to endure hardship and face any danger for the sake of her poor followers was phenomenal.

I regret to hear that she is poor and ill, and hope the sale of your book will give her the relief she so much needs and so well deserves.

Yours truly,
OLIVER JOHNSON.

AUBURN THEOL. SEMINARY,
March 16, 1886.

BY PROFESSOR HOPKINS

The remarkable person who is the subject of the following sketch, has been residing mostly ever since the close of the war in the outskirts of the City of Auburn, during all which time I have been well acquainted with her. She has all the characteristics of the pure African race strongly marked upon her, though from which one of the various tribes that once fed the Barracoons, on the Guinea coast, she derived her indomitable courage and her passionate love of freedom I know not; perhaps from the Fellatas, in whom those traits were predominant.

Harriet lives upon a farm which the twelve hundred dollars given her by Mrs. Bradford from the proceeds of the first edition of this little book, enabled her to redeem from a mortgage held by the late Secretary Seward.

Her household is very likely to consist of several old black people, "bad with the rheumatize," some forlorn wandering woman, and a couple of small images of God cut in ebony. How she manages to feed and clothe herself and them, the Lord best knows. She has too much pride and too much faith to beg. She takes thankfully, but without any great effusiveness of gratitude, whatever God's messengers bring her.

I have never heard that she absolutely lacked. There are some good people in various parts of the country, into whose hearts God sends the thought, from time to time, that Harriet may be at the bottom of the flour sack, or of the potatoes, and the "help in time of need" comes to her.

Harriet's simplicity and ignorance have, in some cases, been imposed upon, very signally in one instance in Auburn, a few years ago; but nobody who knows her has the slightest doubt of her perfect integrity.

The following sketch taken by Mrs. Bradford, chiefly from Harriet's own recollections, which are wonderfully distinct and minute, but also from other corroborative sources, gives but a very imperfect account of what this woman has been.

Her color, and the servile condition in which she was born and reared, have doomed her to obscurity, but a more heroic soul did not breathe in the bosom of Judith or of Jeanne D'Arc.

No fear of the lash, the blood-hound, or the fiery stake, could divert her from her self-imposed task of leading as many as possible of her people "from the land of Egypt, from the house of bondage."

The book is good literature for the black race, or the white race, and though no similar conditions may arise, to test the possibilities that are in any of them, yet the example of this poor slave woman may well stand out before them, and before all people, black or white, to show what a lofty and martyr spirit may accomplish, struggling against overwhelming obstacles.

ON a hot summer's day, perhaps sixty years ago, a group of merry little darkies were rolling and tumbling in the sand in front of the large house of a Southern planter. Their shining skins gleamed in the sun, as they rolled over each other in their play, and their voices, as they chattered together, or shouted in glee, reached even to the cabins of the negro quarter, where the old people groaned in spirit, as they thought of the future of those unconscious young revelers; and their cry went up, "O, Lord, how long!"

Apart from the rest of the children, on the top rail of a fence, holding tight on to the tall gate post, sat a little girl of perhaps thirteen years of age; darker than any of the others, and with a more decided *woolliness* in the hair; a pure unmitigated African. She was not so entirely in a state of nature as the rollers in the dust beneath her; but her only garment was a short woolen skirt, which was tied around her waist, and reached about to her knees. She seemed a dazed and stupid child, and as her head hung upon her breast, she looked up with dull blood-shot eyes towards her young brothers and sisters, without seeming to see them. Bye and bye the eyes closed, and still clinging to the post, she slept. The other children looked up and said to each other, "Look at Hatt, she's done gone off agin!" Tired of their present play ground they trooped off in another direction, but the girl slept on heavily, never losing her hold on the post, or her seat on her perch. Behold here, in the stupid little negro girl, the future deliverer of hundreds of her people; the spy and scout of the Union armies; the devoted hospital nurse; the protector of hunted fugitives; the eloquent speaker in public meetings; the cunning eluder of pursuing man-hunters; the heaven guided pioneer through dangers seen and unseen; in short, as she has well been called, "The Moses of her People."

Here in her thirteenth year she is just recovering from the first terrible effects of an injury inflicted by her master, who in an ungovernable fit of rage threw a heavy weight at the

9

unoffending child, breaking in her skull, and causing a pressure upon her brain, from which in her old age she is suffering still. This pressure it was which caused the fits of somnolency so frequently to come upon her, and which gave her the appearance of being stupid and half-witted in those early years. But that brain which seemed so dull was full of busy thoughts, and her life problem was already trying to work itself out there.

She had heard the shrieks and cries of women who were being flogged in the negro quarter; she had listened to the groaned out prayer, "Oh, Lord, have mercy!" She had already seen two older sisters taken away as part of a chain gang, and they had gone no one knew whither; she had seen the agonized expression on their faces as they turned to take a last look at their "Old Cabin Home"; and had watched them from the top of the fence, as they went off weeping and lamenting, till they were hidden from her sight forever. She saw the hopeless grief of the poor old mother, and the silent despair of the aged father, and already she began to revolve in her mind the question, "Why should such things be?" "Is there no deliverance for my people?"

The sun shone on, and Harriet still slept seated on the fence rail. They, those others, had no anxious dreams of the future, and even the occasional sufferings of the present time caused them but a temporary grief. Plenty to eat, and warm sunshine to bask in, were enough to constitute their happiness; Harriet, however, was not one of these. God had a great work for her to do in the world, and the discipline and hardship through which she passed in her early years, were only preparing her for her after life of adventure and trial; and through these to come out as the Savior and Deliverer of her people, when she came to years of womanhood.

As yet she had seen no "visions," and heard no "voices"; no foreshadowing of her life of toil and privation, of flight before human blood-hounds, of watchings, and hidings, of perils by land, and perils by sea, yea, and of perils by false brethren, or of miraculous deliverance had yet come to her. No hint of the great mission of her life, to guide her people from the land of bondage to the land of freedom. But, "Why should such things be?" and "Is there no help?" These were the questions of her waking hours.

The dilapidated state of things about the "Great House" told truly the story of waning fortunes, and poverty was pressing upon the master. One by one the able-bodied slaves disappeared; some were sold, others hired to other masters. No questions were asked; no information given; they simply disappeared. A "lady," for so she was designated, came driving up to the great house one day, to see if she could find there a young girl to take care of a baby. The lady wished to pay low wages, and so the most stupid and the most incapable of the children on the plantation was chosen to go with her. Harriet, who could command less wages than any other child of her age on the plantation, was therefore put into the wagon without a word of explanation, and driven off to the lady's house. It was not a very fine house, but Harriet had never before been in any dwelling better than the cabins of the negro quarter.

She was engaged as child's nurse, but she soon found that she was expected to be maid of all work by day, as well as child's nurse by night. The first task that was set her was that of sweeping and dusting a parlor. No information was vouchsafed as to the manner of going about this work, but she had often swept out the cabin, and this part of her task was successfully accomplished. Then at once she took the dusting cloth, and wiped off tables, chairs and mantel-piece. The dust, as dust will do, when it has nowhere else to go, at once settled again, and chairs and tables were soon covered with a white coating, telling a terrible tale against Harriet, when her Mistress came in to see how the work progressed. Reproaches, and savage words, fell upon the ears of the frightened child, and she was commanded to do the work all over again. It was done in precisely the same way, as before, with the same result. Then the whip was brought into requisition, and it was laid on with no light hand. Five times before breakfast this process was repeated, when a new actor appeared upon the scene. Miss Emily, a sister of the Mistress, had ben roused from her morning slumber by the sound of the whip, and the screams of the child; and being of a less imperious nature than her sister, she had come in to try to set matters right.

"Why do you whip the child, Susan, for not doing what she has never been taught to do? Leave her to me a few minutes, and you will see that she will soon learn how to sweep and dust a room." Then Miss Emily instructed the child to open the windows, and sweep, then to leave the room, and set the table, while the dust settled; and after that to return and wipe it off. There was no more trouble of that kind. A few words might have set the matter right before; but in those days many a poor slave suffered for the stupidity and obstinacy of a master or mistress, more stupid than themselves.

When the labors, unremitted for a moment, of the long day were over (for this mistress was an economical woman, and intended to get the worth of her money to the uttermost farthing), there was still no rest for the weary child, for there was a cross baby to be rocked continuously, lest it should wake and disturb the mother's rest. The black child sat beside the cradle of the white child, so near the bed, that the lash of the whip would reach her if she ventured for a moment to forget her fatigues and sufferings in sleep. The Mistress reposed upon her bed with the whip on a little shelf over her head. People of color are, unfortunately, so constituted that even if the pressure of a broken skull does not cause a sleep like the sleep of the dead, the need of rest, and the refreshment of slumber after a day of toil, were often felt by them. No doubt, this was a great wrong to their masters, and a cheating them of time which belonged to them, but their slaves did not always look upon it in that light, and tired nature would demand her rights; and so nature and the Mistress had a fight for it.

Rock, rock, went the cradle, and mother and child slept; but alas! the little black hand would sometimes slip down, and the head would droop, and a dream of home and mother would visit the weary one, only to be roughly dispelled by the swift descent of the stinging lash, for the baby had cried out and the mother had been awakened. This is no fictitious tale. That poor neck is even now covered with the scars which sixty years of life have not been able to efface. It may be that she was thus being prepared by the long habit of enforced wakefulness, for the night watches in the woods, and in dens and caves of the earth, when the pursuers were on her track, and the terrified ones were trembling in her shadow. We do not thank *you* for this, cruel woman! for if you did her a service, you did it ignorantly, and only for your own gratification. But Harriet's powers of endurance failed at last, and she was returned to her master, a poor, scarred wreck, nothing but skin and bone, with the words that "She wasn't worth a six-pence."

The poor old mother nursed her back to life, and her naturally good constitution asserted itself, so that as she grew older she began to show signs of the wonderful strength which in after years, when the fugitive slave law was in operation in New York State, enabled her to seize a man from the officers who had him in charge, and while numbers were pursuing her, and the shot was flying like hail about her head, to bear him in her own strong arms beyond the reach of danger.

As soon as she was strong enough for work, Harriet was hired out to a man whose tyranny was worse, if possible, than that of the woman she had left. Now it was out of door drudgery which was put upon her. The labor of the horse and the ox, the lifting of barrels of flour and other heavy weights were given to her; and powerful men often stood astonished to see this woman perform feats of strength from which they shrunk incapable. This cruelty she looks upon as a blessing in disguise (a very questionable shape the blessing took, methinks), for by it she was prepared for after needs.

Still the pressure upon the brain continued, and with the weight half lifted, she would drop off into a state of insensibility, from which even the lash in the hand of a strong man could not rouse her. But if they had only known it, the touch of a gentle hand upon her shoulder, and her name spoken in tones of kindness, would have accomplished what cruelty failed to do.

The day's work must be accomplished, whether the head was racked with pain, and the frame was consumed by fever, or not; but the day came at length when poor Harriet could work no more. The sting of the lash had no power to rouse her now, and the new master finding her a dead weight on his hands, returned the useless piece of property to him who was called her "owner." And while she lay there helpless, this man was bringing other men to look at her, and offering her for sale at the lowest possible price; at the same time setting forth her capabilities, if once she were strong and well again.

Harriet's religious character I have not yet touched upon. Brought up by parents possessed of strong faith in God, she had never known the time, I imagine, when she did not trust Him, and cling to Him, with an all-abiding confidence. She seemed ever to feel the Divine Presence near, and she talked with God "as a man talketh with his friend." Hers was not the religion of a morning and evening prayer at stated times, but when she felt a need, she simply told God of it, and trusted Him to set the matter right.

"And so," she said to me, "as I lay so sick on my bed, from Christmas till March, I was always praying for poor ole master. 'Pears like I didn't do nothing but pray for ole master. 'Oh, Lord, convert ole master'; 'Oh, dear Lord, change dat man's heart, and make him a Christian.' And all the time he was bringing men to look at me, and dey stood there saying what dey would give, and what dey would take, and all I could say was, 'Oh, Lord, convert ole master.' Den I heard dat as soon as I was able to move I was to be sent with my brudders, in the chain-gang to de far South. Then I changed my prayer, and I said, 'Lord, if you ain't never going to change dat man's heart, *kill him,* Lord, and take him out of de way, so he won't do no more mischief.' Next ting I heard ole master was dead; and he died just as he had lived, a wicked, bad man. Oh, den it 'peared like I would give de world full of silver and gold, if I had it, to bring dat pore soul back, I would give *myself;* I would give eberyting! But he was gone, I couldn't pray for him no more."

As she recovered from this long illness, a deeper religious spirit seemed to take possession of her than she had ever experienced before. She literally "prayed without ceasing." "'Pears like, I prayed all de time," she said, "about my work, eberywhere; I was always talking to de Lord. When I went to the horse-trough to wash my face, and took up de water in my hands, I said, 'Oh, Lord, wash me, make me clean.' When I took up de towel to wipe my face and hands, I cried, 'Oh, Lord, for Jesus' sake, wipe away all my sins!' When I took up de broom and began to sweep, I groaned, 'Oh, Lord, whatsoebber sin dere be in my heart, sweep it out, Lord, clar and clean'; but I can't pray no more for pore ole master." No words can describe the pathos of her tones as she broke into these words of earnest supplication.

What was to become of the slaves on this plantation now that the master was dead? Were they all to be scattered and sent to different parts of the country? Harriet had many brothers and sisters, all of whom with the exception of the two, who had gone South with the chain-gang, were living on this plantation, or were hired out to planters not far away. The word passed through the cabins that another owner was coming in, and that none of the slaves were to be sold out of the State. This assurance satisfied the others, but it did not satisfy Harriet. Already the inward monitor was whispering to her, "Arise, flee for your life!" and in the visions of the night she saw the horsemen coming, and heard the shrieks of women and children, as they were being torn from each other, and hurried off no one knew whither.

And beckoning hands were ever motioning her to come, and she seemed to see a line dividing the land of slavery from the land of freedom, and on the other side of that line she saw lovely white ladies waiting to welcome her, and to care for her. Already in her mind her people were the Israelites in the land of Egypt, while far away to the north *somewhere,* was the land of Canaan; but had she as yet any prevision that *she* was to be the Moses who was to be their leader, through clouds of darkness and fear, and fires of tribulation to that promised land? This she never said.

One day there were scared faces seen in the negro quarter, and hurried whispers passed from one to another. No one knew how it had come out, but some one had heard that Harriet and two of her brothers were very soon, perhaps to-day, perhaps to-morrow, to be sent far South with a gang, bought up for plantation work. Harriet was about twenty or twenty-five years old at this time, and the constantly recurring idea of escape at *some-time,* took sudden form that day, and with her usual promptitude of action she was ready to start at once.

She held a hurried consultation with her brothers, in which she so wrought upon their fears, that they expressed themselves as willing to start with her that very night, for that far North, where, could they reach it in safety, freedom awaited them. But she must first give some intimation of her purpose to the friends she was to leave behind, so that even if not understood at the time, it might be remembered afterward as her intended farewell. Slaves must not be seen talking together, and so it came about that their communication was often made by singing, and the words of their familiar hymns, telling of the heavenly journey, and the land of Canaan, while they did not attract the attention of the masters, conveyed to their brethren and sisters in bondage something more than met the ear. And so she sang, accompanying the words, when for a moment unwatched, with a meaning look to one and another:

> "When dat ar ole chariot comes,
>   I'm gwine to lebe you,
> I'm boun' for de promised land,
>   Frien's, I'm gwine to lebe you."

Again, as she passed the doors of the different cabins, she lifted up her well-known voice; and many a dusky face appeared at door or window, with a wondering or scared expression; and thus she continued:

> "I'm sorry, frien's, to lebe you,
>   Farewell! oh, farewell!
> But I'll meet you in de mornin',
>   Farewell! oh, farewell!

> "I'll meet you in de mornin',
>   When you reach de promised land;
> On de oder side of Jordan,
>   For I'm boun' for de promised land."

The brothers started with her, but the way was strange, the north was far away, and all unknown, the masters would pursue and recapture them, and their fate would be worse than ever before; and so they broke away from her, and bidding her good-bye, they hastened back to the known horrors of slavery, and the dread of that which was worse.

Harriet was now left alone, but after watching the retreating forms of her brothers, she turned her face toward the north, and fixing her eyes on the guiding star, and committing her way unto the Lord, she started again upon her long, lonely journey. Her farewell song was long remembered in the cabins, and the old mother sat and wept for her lost child. No intimation had been given her of Harriet's intention, for the old woman was of a most impulsive disposition, and her cries and lamentations would have made known to all within hearing Harriet's intended escape. And so, with only the North Star for her guide, our heroine started on the way to liberty. "For," said she, "I had reasoned dis out in my mind; there was one of two things I had a *right* to, liberty, or death; if I could not have one, I would have de oder; for no man should take me alive; I should fight for my liberty as long as my strength lasted, and when de time came for me to go, de Lord would let dem take me."

And so without money, and without friends, she started on through unknown regions; walking by night, hiding by day, but always conscious of an invisible pillar of cloud by day, and of fire by night, under the guidance of which she journeyed or rested. Without knowing whom to trust, or how near the pursuers might be, she carefully felt her way, and by her native cunning, or by God given wisdom, she managed to apply to the right people for food, and sometimes for shelter; though often her bed was only the cold ground, and her watchers the stars of night.

After many long and weary days of travel, she found that she had passed the magic line, which then divided the land of bondage from the land of freedom. But where were the lovely white ladies whom in her visions she had seen, who, with arms outstretched, welcomed her to their hearts and homes? All these visions proved deceitful: she was more alone than ever; but she had crossed the line; no one could take her now, and she would never call any man "Master" more.

"I looked at my hands," she said, "to see if I was de same person now I was free. Dere was such a glory ober eberything, de sun came like gold trou de trees, and ober de fields, and I felt

like I was in heaven." But then came the bitter drop in the cup
of joy. She was alone, and her kindred were in slavery, and not
one of them had the courage to dare what she had dared. Unless
she made the effort to liberate them she would never see them
more, or even know their fate.

"I knew of a man," she said, "who was sent to the State Prison
for twenty-five years. All these years he was always thinking of
his home, and counting by years, months, and days, the time till
he should be free, and see his family and friends once more.
The years roll on, the time of imprisonment is over, the man is
free. He leaves the prison gates, he makes his way to his old
home, but his old home is not there. The house in which he had
dwelt in his childhood had been torn down, and a new one had
been put up in its place; his family were gone, their very name
was forgotten, there was no one to take him by the hand to welcome him back to life."

"So it was wid me," said Harriet, "I had crossed de line of
which I had so long been dreaming. I was free; but dere was no
one to welcome me to de land of freedom, I was a stranger in a
strange land, and my home after all was down in de old cabin
quarter, wid de ole folks, and my brudders and sisters. But to dis
solemn resolution I came; I was free, and dey should be free
also; I would make a home for dem in de North, and de Lord
helping me, I would bring dem all dere. Oh, how I prayed den,
lying all alone on de cold, damp ground; "Oh, dear Lord," I said,
"I haint got no friend but *you*. Come to my help, Lord, for I'm
in trouble!"

It would be impossible here to give a detailed account of the
journeys and labors of this intrepid woman for the redemption
of her kindred and friends, during the years that followed.
Those years were spent in work, almost by night and day, with
the one object of the rescue of her people from slavery. All her
wages were laid away with this sole purpose, and as soon as a
sufficient amount was secured, she disappeared from her
Northern home, and as suddenly and mysteriously she appeared
some dark night at the door of one of the cabins on a plantation,
where a trembling band of fugitives, forewarned as to time and
place, were anxiously awaiting their deliverer. Then she piloted

them North, traveling by night, hiding by day, scaling the mountains, fording the rivers, threading the forests, lying concealed as the pursuers passed them. She, carrying the babies, drugged with paregoric, in a basket on her arm. So she went *nineteen* times, and so she brought away over three hundred pieces of living and breathing "property," with God given souls.

The way was so toilsome over the rugged mountain passes, that often the *men* who followed her would give out, and footsore, and bleeding, they would drop on the ground, groaning that they could not take another step. They would lie there and die, or if strength came back, they would return on their steps, and seek their old homes again. Then the revolver carried by this bold and daring pioneer, would come out, while pointing it at their heads she would say, "Dead niggers tell no tales; you go on or die!" And by this heroic treatment she compelled them to drag their weary limbs along on their northward journey.

But the pursuers were after them. A reward of $40,000 was offered by the slave-holders of the region from whence so many slaves had been spirited away, for the head of the woman who appeared so mysteriously, and enticed away their property, from under the very eyes of its owners. Our sagacious heroine has been in the car, having sent her frightened party round by some so-called "Under-ground Railway," and has heard this advertisement, which was posted over her head, read by others of the passengers. She never could read or write herself, but knowing that suspicion would be likely to fall upon any black woman traveling North, she would turn at the next station, and journey towards the South. Who would suspect a fugitive with such a price set upon her head, of rushing at railway speed into the jaws of destruction? With a daring almost heedless, she went even to the very village where she would be most likely to meet one of the masters to whom she had been hired; and having stopped at the Market and bought a pair of live fowls, she went along the street with her sun-bonnet well over her face, and with the bent and decrepit air of an aged woman. Suddenly on turning a corner, she spied her old master coming towards her. She pulled the string which tied the legs of the chickens; they began to flutter and scream, and as her master passed, she was stooping and busily engaged in attending to the fluttering fowls. And he went on his way, little thinking that he was brushing the very garments of the woman who had dared to steal herself, and others of his belongings.

At one time the pursuit was very close and vigorous. The woods were scoured in all directions, every house was visited, and every person stopped and questioned as to a band of black fugitives, known to be fleeing through that part of the country. Harriet had a large party with her then; the children were sleeping the sound sleep that opium gives; but all the others were on the alert, each one hidden behind his own tree, and silent as death. They had been long without food, and were nearly famished; and as the pursuers seemed to have passed on, Harriet decided to make the attempt to reach a certain "station of the underground railroad" well known to her; and procure food for her starving party. Under cover of the darkness, she started, leaving a cowering and trembling group in the woods, to whom a fluttering leaf, or a moving animal, were a sound of dread, bringing their hearts into their throats. How long she is away! Has she been caught and carried off, and if so what is to become of them? Hark! there is a sound of singing in the distance, coming nearer and nearer.

And these are the words of the unseen singer, which I wish I could give you as I have so often heard them sung by herself:

> Hail, oh hail, ye happy spirits,
>   Death no more shall make you fear,
> Grief nor sorrow, pain nor anguish,
>   Shall no more distress you dere.
>
> Around Him are ten thousand angels,
>   Always ready to obey command;
> Dey are always hovering round you,
>   Till you reach de heavenly land.
>
> Jesus, Jesus will go wid you,
>   He will lead you to his throne;
> He who died, has gone before you,
>   Trod de wine-press all alone.

> He whose thunders shake creation,
>   He who bids de planets roll;
> He who rides upon the tempest,
>   And whose scepter sways de whole.
>
> Dark and thorny is de pathway,
>   Where de pilgrim makes his ways;
> But beyond dis vale of sorrow,
>   Lie de fields of endless days.

The air sung to these words was so wild, so full of plaintive minor strains, and unexpected quavers, that I would defy any white person to learn it, and often as I heard it, it was to me a constant surprise. Up and down the road she passes to see if the coast is clear, and then to make them certain that it is *their* leader who is coming, she breaks out into the plaintive strains of the song, forbidden to her people at the South, but which she and her followers delight to sing together:

> Oh go down, Moses,
>   Way down into Egypt's land,
> Tell old Pharaoh,
>   Let my people go.
>
> Oh Pharaoh said he would go cross,
>   Let my people go,
> And don't get lost in de wilderness,
>   Let my people go.
>
> Oh go down, Moses,
>   Way down into Egypt's land,
> Tell old Pharaoh,
>   Let my people go.
>
> You may hinder me here, but you can't up dere,
>   Let my people go,
> He sits in de Hebben and answers prayer,
>   Let my people go!
>
> Oh go down, Moses,
>   Way down into Egypt's land,
> Tell old Pharaoh,
>   Let my people go.

And then she enters the recesses of the wood, carrying hope and comfort to the anxious watchers there. One by one they steal out from their hiding places, and are fed and strengthened for another night's journey.

And so by night travel, by signals, by threatenings, by encouragement, through watchings and fastings, and I may say by direct interpositions of Providence, and miraculous deliverances, she brought her people to what was then their land of Canaan; the State of New York. But alas! this State did not continue to be their refuge. For in 1850, I think, the Fugitive Slave Law was put in force, which bound the people north of Mason and Dixon's line, to return to bondage any fugitive found in their territories.

"After that," said Harriet, "I wouldn't trust Uncle Sam wid my people no longer, but I brought 'em all clar off to Canada."

On her seventh or eighth journey, she brought with her a band of fugitives, among whom was a very remarkable man, whom I knew only by the name of "Joe." Joe was a noble specimen of a negro, enormously tall, and of splendid muscular development. He had been hired out by his master to another planter, for whom he had worked for six years, saving him all the expense of an overseer, and taking all trouble off from his hands. He was such a very valuable piece of property, and had become so absolutely necessary to the planter to whom he was hired, that he determined to buy him at any cost. His old master held him proportionately high. But by paying one thousand dollars down, and promising to pay another thousand in a certain time, the purchase was made, and this chattel passed over into the hands of a new owner.

The morning after the purchase was completed, the new master came riding down on a tall, powerful horse into the negro quarter, with a strong new rawhide in his hand, and stopping before Joe's cabin, called to him to come out. Joe was just eating his breakfast, but with ready obedience, he hastened out at the summons. Slave as he was, and accustomed to scenes of brutality, he was surprised when the order came, "Now, Joe, strip, and take a licking." Naturally enough, he demurred at first, and thought of resisting the order; but he called to mind a scene he had witnessed a few days before in the field, the particulars of which are too horrible to be given here, and he thought it the wisest course to submit; but first he tried a gentle remonstrance.

"Mas'r," said he, "habn't I always been faithful to you? Habn't I worked through sun an' rain, early in de mornin' an' late at night; habn't I saved you an oberseer by doin' his work? Hab you anything to complain agin me?"

"No, Joe, I have no complaint to make of you. You're a good nigger, an' you've always worked well. But you belong to *me* now; you're *my* nigger, and the first lesson my niggers have to learn is that I am master and they belong to me, and are never to resist anything I order them to do. So I always begin by giving them a good licking. Now strip and take it."

Joe saw that there was no help for him, and that for the time he must submit. He stripped off his clothing, and took his flogging without a word, but as he drew his shirt up over his torn and bleeding back, he said to himself: "Dis is de first an' de last." As soon as he was able he took a boat, and under cover of the night, rowed down the river, and made his way to the cabin of "Old Ben," Harriet's father, and said to him: "Nex' time *Moses* comes, let me know."

It was not long after this time, that the mysterious woman appeared—the woman on whom no one could lay his finger— and men, women, and children began to disappear from the plantations. One fine morning Joe was missing, and call as loud as he might, the master's voice had no power to bring him forth. Joe had certainly fled; and his brother William was gone, and Peter and Eliza. From other plantations other slaves were missing, and before their masters were awake to the fact, the party of fugitives, following their intrepid leader, were far on their way towards liberty.

The adventures of this escaping party would of themselves fill a volume. They hid in potato holes by day, while their pursuers passed within a few feet of them; they were passed along by friends in various disguises; they scattered and separated; some traveling by boat, some by wagons, some by cars, others on foot, to meet at some specified station of the under-ground railroad. They met at the house of Sam Green,° the man who was afterwards sent to prison for ten years for having a copy of "Uncle Tom's Cabin" in his house. And so, hunted and hiding and wandering, they found themselves at last at the entrance of the long bridge which crosses the river at Wilmington, Delaware.

No time had been lost in posting up advertisements and offering rewards for the capture of these fugitives; for Joe in particular the reward offered was very high. First a thousand dollars, then fifteen hundred, and then two thousand, "an' all expenses clar an' clean for his body in Easton Jail." This high reward stimulated the efforts of the officers who were usually on the lookout for escaping fugitives, and the added rewards for others of the party, and the high price set on Harriet's head, filled the woods and highways with eager hunters after human prey. When Harriet and her companions approached the long Wilmington Bridge, a warning was given them by some secret friend, that the advertisements were up, and the bridge was guarded by police officers. Quick as lightning the plans were formed in her ready brain, and the terrified party were separated and hidden in the houses of different friends, till her arrangements for their further journey were completed.

There was at that time residing in Wilmington an old Quaker, whom I may call *my* "friend," for though I never saw his face, I have had correspondence with him in reference to Harriet and her followers. This man, whose name was Thomas Garrett, and

---

°In mentioning to me the circumstances of Sam Green's imprisonment, Harriet, who had no acquaintance with books, merely mentioned the fact as it had come to her own knowledge. But I have lately come across a book in the Astor Library which confirms the story precisely as she stated it. It is in a book by Rev. John Dixon Long, of Philadelphia. He says, "Samuel Green, a free colored man of Dorchester County, Maryland, was sentenced to ten years' confinement in the Maryland State Prison, at the spring term of the County Court held in Cambridge, Md.

"What was the crime imputed to this man, born on American soil, a man of good moral character, a local preacher in the Methodist Episcopal Church; a husband and a father? Simply this: A copy of 'Uncle Tom's Cabin' *had been found in his possession.* It was not proved that he had ever read it to the colored people."

who was well known in those days to the friends of the slave, was a man of a wonderfully large and generous heart, through whose hands during those days of distress and horror, no less than three thousand self-emancipated men, women and children passed on their way to freedom. He gave heart, hand, and means to aid these poor fugitives, and to our brave Harriet he often rendered most efficient help in her journeys back and forth.

He was the proprietor of a very large shoe establishment; and not one of these poor travelers ever left his house without a present of a new pair of shoes and other needed help. No sooner had this good man received intelligence of the condition of these poor creatures, than he devised a plan to elude the vigilance of the officers in pursuit, and bring Harriet and her party across the bridge. Two wagons filled with bricklayers were engaged, and sent over; this was a common sight there, and caused no remark. They went across the bridge singing and shouting, and it was not an unexpected thing that they should return as they went. After nightfall (and, fortunately, the night was very dark) the same wagons recrossed the bridge, but with an unlooked-for addition to their party. The fugitives were lying close together on the bottom of the wagons; the bricklayers were on the seats, still singing and shouting; and so they passed the guards, who were all unsuspicious of the nature of the load contained in the wagons, or of the amount of property thus escaping their hands.

The good man, Thomas Garrett, who was in a very feeble state of health when he last wrote me, and has now gone to his reward, supplied them with all needed comforts, and sent them on their way refreshed, and with renewed courage. And Harriet here set up her Ebenezer, saying, "Thus far hath the Lord helped me!" But many a danger, and many a fright, and many a deliverance awaited them, before they reached the city of New York. And even there they were not safe, for the Fugitive Slave Law was in operation, and their only refuge was Canada, which was now their promised land.

They finally reached New York in safety: and this goes almost without saying, for I may as well mention here that of the three hundred and more fugitives whom Harriet piloted from slavery, not one was ever recaptured, though all the cunning and skill of white men, backed by offered rewards of large sums of money, were brought into requisition for their recovery.

As they entered the anti-slavery office in New York, Mr. Oliver Johnson rose up and exclaimed, "Well, Joe, I am glad to see the man who is worth $2,000 to his master." At this Joe's heart sank. "Oh, Mas'r, how did you know me!" he panted. "Here is the advertisement in our office," said Mr. Johnson, "and the description is so close that no one could mistake it." And had he come through all these perils, had he traveled by day and night, and suffered cold and hunger, and lived in constant fear and dread, to find that far off here in New York State, he was recognized at once by the advertisement? How, then, was he ever to reach Canada?

"And how far off is Canada?" he asked. He was shown the map of New York State, and the track of the railroad, for more than three hundred miles to Niagara, where he would cross the river, and be free. But the way seemed long and full of dangers. They were surely safer on their own tired feet, where they might hide in forests and ditches, and take refuge in the friendly underground stations; but here, where this large party would be together in the cars, surely suspicion would fall upon them, and they would be seized and carried back. But Harriet encouraged him in her cheery way. He must not give up now. "De Lord had been with them in six troubles, and he would not desert them in de seventh." And there was nothing to do but to go on. As Moses spoke to the children of Israel, when compassed before and behind by dangers, so she spake to her people, that they should "go forward."

Up to this time, as they traveled they had talked and sung hymns together, like Pilgrim and his friends, and Joe's voice was the loudest and sweetest among them; but now he hanged his harp upon the willows, and could sing the Lord's songs no more.

"From dat time," in Harriet's language, "Joe was silent; he talked no more; he sang no more; he sat wid his head on his hand, an' nobody could 'rouse him, nor make him take any intrust in anything."

They passed along in safety through New York State, and at length found themselves approaching the Suspension Bridge. They could see the promised land on the other side. The uninviting plains of Canada seemed to them,

"Sweet fields beyond the swelling flood,
All dressed in living green;"

but they were not safe yet. Until they reached the center of the bridge, they were still in the power of their pursuers, who might at any pause enter the car, and armed with the power of the law, drag them back to slavery. The rest of the party were happy and excited; they were simple, ignorant creatures, and having implicit trust in their leader, they felt safe when with her, and no immediate danger threatened them. But Joe was of a different mould. He sat silent and sad, always thinking of the horrors that awaited him if recaptured. As it happened, all the other passengers were people who sympathized with them, understanding them to be a band of fugitives, and they listened with tears, as Harriet and all except poor Joe lifted up their voices and sang:

I'm on the way to Canada,
   That cold and dreary land,
De sad effects of slavery,
   I can't no longer stand;
I've served my Master all my days,
   Widout a dime reward,
And now I'm forced to run away,
   To flee de lash, abroad;
Farewell, ole Master, don't think hard of me,
I'm traveling on to Canada, where all de slaves are free.

De hounds are baying on my track,
   Ole Master comes behind,
Resolved that he will bring me back,
   Before I cross the line;
I'm now embarked for yonder shore,
   Where a man's a *man* by law,
De iron horse will bear me o'er,
   To "shake de lion's paw;"
Oh, righteous Father, wilt thou not pity me,
And help me on to Canada, where all de slaves are free.

> Oh I heard Queen Victoria say,
>   That if we would forsake,
> Our native land of slavery,
>   And come across de lake;
> Dat she was standing on de shore,
>   Wid arms extended wide,
> To give us all a peaceful home,
>   Beyond de rolling tide;
> Farewell, ole Master, don't think hard of me,
> I'm traveling on to Canada, where all de slaves are free.

No doubt the simple creatures with her expected to cross a wide lake instead of a rapid river, and to see Queen Victoria with her crown upon her head, waiting with arms extended wide, to fold them all in her embrace. There was now but "one wide river to cross," and the cars rolled on to the bridge. In the distance was heard the roar of the mighty cataract, and now as they neared the center of the bridge, the falls might be clearly seen. Harriet was anxious to have her companions see this wonderful sight, and succeeded in bringing all to the windows, except Joe. But Joe still sat with his head on his hands, and not even the wonders of Niagara could draw him from his melancholy musings. At length as Harriet knew by the rise of the center of the bridge, and the descent immediately after, the line of danger was passed; she sprang across to Joe's side of the car, and shook him almost out of his seat, as she shouted, "Joe! you've shook de lion's paw!" This was her phrase for having entered on the dominions of England. But Joe did not understand this figurative expression. Then she shook him again, and put it more plainly, "Joe, you're in Queen Victoria's dominions! You're a free man!"

Then Joe arose. His head went up, he raised his hands on high, and his eyes, streaming with tears, to heaven, and then he began to sing and shout:

> "Glory to God and Jesus too,
>   One more soul got safe;
> Oh, go and carry the news,
>   One more soul got safe."

"Joe, come and look at the falls!"

"Glory to God and Jesus too,
One more soul got safe."

"Joe! it's your last chance. Come and see de falls!"

"Glory to God and Jesus too,
One more soul got safe."

And this was all the answer. The train stopped on the other side; and the first feet to touch British soil, after those of the conductor, were those of poor Joe.

Loud roared the waters of Niagara, but louder still ascended the Anthem of praise from the overflowing heart of the free-man. And can we doubt that the strain was taken up by angel voices and echoed and re-echoed through the vaults of heaven:

Glory to God in the highest,
Glory to God and Jesus too
For all these souls now safe.

"The white ladies and gentlemen gathered round him," said Harriet, "till I couldn't see Joe for the crowd, only I heard his voice singing, 'Glory to God and Jesus too,' louder than ever." A sweet young lady reached over her fine cambric handkerchief to him, and as Joe wiped the great tears off his face, he said, "Tank de Lord! dere's only one more journey for me now, and dat's to Hebben!" As we bid farewell to Joe here, I may as well say that Harriet saw him several times after that, a happy and industri-ous freeman in Canada.°

°In my recent interview with Mr. Oliver Johnson he told me of an interesting incident in the life of the good man, Thomas Garrett.

He was tried twice for assisting in the escape of fugitive slaves, and was fined so heavily that everything he possessed was taken from him and sold to pay the fine. At the age of sixty he was left without a penny, but he went bravely to work, and in some measure regained his fortune; all the time aid-ing, in every way possible, all stray fugitives who applied to him for help.

Again he was arrested, tried, and heavily fined, and as the Judge of the United States Court pronounced the sentence, he said, in a solemn manner: "Garrett, let this be a lesson to you, not to interfere hereafter with the cause of justice, by helping off runaway negroes."—(cont.)

On one of her journeys to the North, as she was piloting a company of refugees, Harriet came, just as morning broke, to a town, where a colored man had lived whose house had been one of her stations of the under-ground, or unseen railroad. They reached the house, and leaving her party huddled together in the middle of the street, in a pouring rain, Harriet went to the door, and gave the peculiar rap which was her customary signal to her friends. There was not the usual ready response, and she was obliged to repeat the signal several times. At length a window was raised, and the head of a *white man* appeared, with the gruff question, "Who are you?" and "What do you want?" Harriet asked after her friend, and was told that he had been obliged to leave for "harboring niggers."

Here was an unforeseen trouble; day was breaking, and daylight was the enemy of the hunted and flying fugitives. Their faithful leader stood one moment in the street, and in that moment she had flashed a message quicker than that of the telegraph to her unseen Protector, and the answer came as quickly; in a suggestion to her of an almost forgotten place of refuge. Outside of the town there was a little island in a swamp, where the grass grew tall and rank, and where no human being could be suspected of seeking a hiding place. To this spot she conducted her party; she waded the swamp, carrying in a basket two well-drugged babies (these were a pair of little twins, whom I have since seen well grown young women), and the rest of the company following. She ordered them to lie down in the tall, wet grass, and here she prayed again, and waited for deliverance. The poor creatures were all cold, and wet, and hungry,

---

The old man, who had stood to receive his sentence, here raised his head, and fixing his eyes on "the Court," he said:

"Judge—thee hasn't left me a dollar, but I wish to say to thee, and to all in this court room, that if anyone knows of a fugitive who wants a shelter, and a friend, *send him to Thomas Garrett,* and he will befriend him !"

Not Luther before the Council at Worms was grander than this brave old man in his unswerving adherence to principle. In those days that tried men's souls there were many men like this old Quaker, and many women too, who would have gone cheerfully to the fire and the stake, for the cause of suffering humanity; men and women *these* "of whom the world was not worthy."

and Harriet did not dare to leave them to get supplies; for no doubt the man at whose house she had knocked, had given the alarm in the town; and officers might be on the watch for them. They were truly in a wretched condition, but Harriet's faith never wavered, her silent prayer still ascended, and she confidently expected help from some quarter or other.

It was after dusk when a man came slowly walking along the solid pathway on the edge of the swamp. He was clad in the garb of a Quaker; and proved to be a "friend" in need and indeed; he seemed to be talking to himself, but ears quickened by sharp practice caught the words he was saying:

"My wagon stands in the barn-yard of the next farm across the way. The horse is in the stable; the harness hangs on a nail." And the man was gone. Night fell, and Harriet stole forth to the place designated. Not only a wagon, but a wagon well provisioned stood in the yard; and before many minutes the party were rescued from their wretched position, and were on their way rejoicing, to the next town. Here dwelt a Quaker whom Harriet knew, and he readily took charge of the horse and wagon, and no doubt returned them to their owner. How the good man who thus came to their rescue had received any intimation of their being in the neighborhood Harriet never knew. But these sudden deliverances never seemed to strike her as at all strange or mysterious; her prayer was the prayer of faith, and she *expected* an answer.

At one time, as she was on her way South for a party of slaves, she was stopped not far from the southern shore of the Chesapeake Bay, by a young woman, who had been for some days in hiding, and was anxiously watching for "Moses," who was soon expected to pass that way.

This girl was a young and pretty Mulatto, named Tilly, she had been lady's maid and dressmaker, for her Mistress. She was engaged to a young man from another plantation, but he had joined one of Harriet's parties, and gone North. Tilly was to have gone also at that time, but had found it impossible to get away. Now she had learned that it was her Master's intention to give her to a Negro of his own for his wife; and in fear and desperation, she made a strike for freedom. Friends had concealed her, and all had been on the watch for Moses.

The distress and excitement of the poor creature was so great, and she begged and implored in such agonized tones that Harriet would just see her safe to Baltimore, where she knew of friends who would harbor her, and help her on her way, that Harriet determined to turn about, and endeavor to take the poor girl thus far on her Northward journey.

They reached the shore of Chesapeake Bay too late to leave that night, and were obliged to hide for a night and day in the loft of an old out-house, where every sound caused poor Tilly to tremble as if she had an ague fit. When the time for the boat to leave arrived, a sad disappointment awaited them. The boat on which they had expected to leave was disabled, and another boat was to take its place. At that time, according to the law of Slavery, no Negro could leave his Master's land, or travel anywhere, without a pass, properly signed by his owner. Of course this poor fugitive had no pass; and Harriet's passes were her own wits; but among her many friends, there was one who seemed to have influence with the clerk of the boat, on which she expected to take passage; and she was the bearer of a note requesting, or commanding him to take these two women to the end of his route, asking no questions.

Now here was an unforeseen difficulty; the boat was not going; the clerk was not there; all on the other boat were strangers. But forward they must go, trusting in Providence. As they walked down to the boat, a gang of lazy white men standing together, began to make comments on their appearance.

"Too many likely looking Niggers traveling North, about these days." "Wonder if these wenches have got a pass." "Where you going, you two?" Tilly trembled and cowered, and clung to her protector, but Harriet put on a bold front, and holding the note given her by her friend in her hand, and supporting her terrified charge, she walked by the men, taking no notice of their insults.

They joined the stream of people going up to get their tickets, but when Harriet asked for hers, the clerk eyed her suspiciously, and said: "You just stand aside, you two; I'll attend to your case bye and bye."

Harriet led the young girl to the bow of the boat, where they were alone, and here, having no other help, she, as was her custom, addressed herself to the Lord. Kneeling on the seat, and supporting her head on her hands, and fixing her eyes on the waters of the bay, she groaned:

"Oh, Lord! You've been wid me in six troubles, *don't* desert me in the seventh!"

"Moses! Moses!" cried Tilly, pulling her by the sleeve. "Do go and see if you can't get tickets now."

"Oh, Lord! You've been wid me in six troubles, *don't* desert me in the seventh."

And so Harriet's story goes on in her peculiarly graphic manner, till at length in terror Tilly exclaimed:

"Oh, Moses! the man is coming. What shall we do?"

"Oh, Lord, you've been wid me in six troubles!"

Here the clerk touched her on the shoulder, and Tilly thought their time had come, but all he said was:

"You can come now and get your tickets," and their troubles were over.

What changed this man from his former suspicious and antagonistic aspect, Harriet never knew. Of course she said it was "de Lord," but as to the agency he used, she never troubled herself to inquire. She *expected* deliverance when she prayed, unless the Lord had ordered otherwise, and in that case she was perfectly willing to accept the Divine decree.

When surprise was expressed at her courage and daring, or at her unexpected deliverances, she would always reply: "Don't, I tell you, Missus, 'twan't *me*, 'twas *de Lord!* Jes' so long as he wanted to use me, he would take keer of me, an' when he didn't want me no longer, I was ready to go; I always tole him, I'm gwine to hole stiddy on to you, an' you've got to see me trou."

There came a time when Harriet, who had already brought away as many of her family as she could reach, besides all others who would trust themselves to her care, became much troubled in "spirit" about three of her brothers, having had an intimation of some kind that danger was impending over them. With her usual wonderful cunning, she employed a friend to write a letter for her to a man named Jacob Jackson, who lived near the plantation where these brothers were at that time the hired slaves.

Jacob Jackson was a free negro, who could both read and

write, and who was under suspicion just then of having a hand in the disappearance of colored "property." It was necessary, therefore, to exercise great caution in writing to him, on his own account as well as that of the writer, and those whom she wished to aid. Jacob had an adopted son, William Henry Jackson, also free, who had come North. Harriet determined to sign her letter with William Henry's name, feeling sure that Jacob would be clever enough to understand by her peculiar phraseology, the meaning she intended to convey.

Therefore, after speaking of indifferent matters, the letter went on: "Read my letter to the old folks, and give my love to them, and tell my brothers to be always *watching unto prayer,* and when *the good old ship of Zion comes along, to be ready to step on board.*" This letter was signed "William Henry Jackson."

Jacob was not allowed to have his letters in those days, until the self-elected inspectors of correspondence had had the perusal of them, and consulted over their secret meaning. These wiseacres therefore assembled, wiped their glasses carefully, put them on, and proceeded to examine this suspicious document. What it meant they could not imagine. William Henry Jackson had no parents, or brothers, and the letter was incomprehensible. Study as they might, no light dawned upon them, but their suspicions became stronger, and they were sure the letter meant mischief.

White genius having exhausted itself, black genius was brought into requisition. Jacob was sent for, and the letter was placed in his hands. He read between the lines, and comprehended the hidden meaning at once. "Moses" had dictated this letter, and Moses was coming. The brothers must be on the watch, and ready to join her at a moment's warning. But Moses must hurry, for the word had gone forth that the brothers were to be sent South, and the chain-gang was being collected.

Jacob read the letter slowly, threw it down, and said: "Dat letter can't be meant for me no how; I can't make head or tail of it." And he walked off and took immediate measures to let Harriet's brothers know that she was on the way, and they must be ready at the given signal to start for the North.

It was the day before Christmas when Harriet arrived, and the brothers were to have started on the day after Christmas for the South. They started on Christmas-day, but with their faces turned in another direction, and instead of the chain-gang and the whip, they had the North Star for their guide, and the Moses of her people for their leader.

As usual, this mysterious woman appeared suddenly, and word was conveyed to the brothers that they were to be at Old Ben's cabin on Saturday night, ready to start. "Old Ben" was their father, and as the parents were not of much use now, Harriet was pretty certain that they would not be sent away, and so she left them till she had rescued the younger and more valuable members of the family.

Quite a number had assembled at the cabin when the hour came for starting, but one brother was missing. Something had detained John; but when the time for starting had struck, Harriet's word was "forward," and she "nebber waited for no one."

Poor John was ready to start from his cabin in the negro quarter when his wife was taken ill, and in an hour or two another little heir to the blessings of slavery had come into the world.

John must go off for a "Granny," and being a faithful, affectionate creature, he could not leave his wife under the present circumstances.

After the birth of the child he determined to start. The North and freedom, or the South and life-long slavery, were the alternatives before him; and this was his last chance. If he once reached the North, he hoped with the help of Moses to bring his wife and children there.

Again and again he tried to start out of the door, but a watchful eye was on him, and he was always arrested by the question, "Where you gwine, John?" His wife had not been informed of the danger hanging over his head, but she knew he was uneasy, and she feared he was meditating a plan of escape. John told her he was going to try to get hired out on Christmas to another man, as that was the day on which such changes were made.

He left the house but stood near the window listening. He heard his wife sobbing and moaning, and not being able to endure it he went back to her. "Oh, John!" she cried, "you's gwine to lebe me! I know it! but wherebber you go, John, don't forget me an' de little children."

John assured her that wherever he went she should come. He might not come for her, but he would send Moses, and then he hurried away. He had many miles to walk to his old father's cabin, where he knew the others would be waiting for him, and at daybreak he overtook them in the "fodder house," not far from the home of the old people.

At that time Harriet had not seen her mother for six years, but she did not dare to let her know that four of her children were so near her on their way to the North, for she would have raised such an uproar in her efforts to detain them, that the whole neighborhood would have been aroused.

The poor old woman had been expecting her sons to spend Christmas with her as usual. She had been hard at work in preparation for their arrival. The fatted pig had been killed, and had been converted into every form possible to the flesh of swine; pork, bacon and sausages were ready, but the boys did not come, and there she sat watching and waiting.

In the night when Harriet with two of her brothers, and two other fugitives who had joined them arrived at the "fodder house," they were exhausted and well-nigh famished. They sent the two strange men up to the cabin to try to rouse "Old Ben," but not to let their mother know that her children were so near her.

The men succeeded in rousing Old Ben, who came out quietly, and as soon as he heard their story, went back into the house, gathered together a quantity of provisions, and came down to the fodder house. He placed the provisions inside the door, saying a few words of welcome to his children, but taking care *not to see them*. "I know what'll come of dis," he said, "an' I ain't gwine to see my chillen, no how." The close espionage under which these poor creatures dwelt, engendered in them a cunning and artifice, which to them seemed only a fair and right attempt on their part, to cope with power and cruelty constantly in force against them.

Up among the ears of corn lay the old man's children, and one of them he had not seen for six years. It rained in torrents all that Sunday, and there they lay among the corn, for they could not start till night. At about daybreak John had joined them. There were wide chinks in the boards of the fodder house, and through these they could see the cabin of the old folks, now quite alone in their old age. All day long, every few minutes, they would see the old woman come out, and shading her eyes with her hand, take a long look down the road to see if "de boys" were coming, and then with a sad and disappointed air she would turn back into the cabin, and they could almost hear her sigh as she did so.

What had become of the boys? Had they been sold off down South? Had they tried to escape and been retaken? Would she never see them or hear of them more?

I have often heard it said by Southern people that "niggers had no feeling; they did not care when their children were taken from them." I have seen enough of them to know that their love for their offspring is quite equal to that of the "superior race," and it is enough to hear the tale of Harriet's endurance and self-sacrifice to rescue her brothers and sisters, to convince one that a heart, truer and more loving than that of many a white woman, dwelt in her bosom. I am quite willing to acknowledge that she was almost an anomaly among her people, but I have known many of her family, and so far as I can judge they all seem to be peculiarly intelligent, upright and religious people, and to have a strong feeling of family affection. There may be many among the colored race like them; certainly all should not be judged by the idle, miserable darkies who have swarmed about Washington and other cities since the War.

Two or three times while the group of fugitives were concealed in this loft of the fodder house, the old man came down and pushed food inside the door, and after nightfall he came again to accompany his children as far as he dared, upon their journey. When he reached the fodder house, he tied a handkerchief tight about his eyes, and one of his sons taking him by one arm, and Harriet taking him by the other, they went on their way talking in low tones together, asking and answering questions as to relatives and friends.

The time of parting came, and they bade him farewell, and left him standing in the middle of the road. When he could no longer hear their footsteps he turned back, and taking the handkerchief from his eyes, he hastened home.

But before Harriet and her brothers left, they had gone up to the cabin during the evening to take a silent farewell of the poor old mother. Through the little window of the cabin they saw her sitting by the fire, her head on her hand, rocking back and forth, as was her way when she was in great trouble; praying, no doubt, and wondering what had become of her children, and what new evil had befallen them.

With streaming eyes, they watched her for ten or fifteen minutes; but time was precious, and they must reach their next underground station before daylight, and so they turned sadly away.

When Christmas was over, and the men had not returned, there began to be no small stir in the plantation from which they had escaped. The first place to search, of course, was the home of the old people. At the "Big House" nothing had been seen of them. The master said "they had generally come up there to see the house servants, when they came for Christmas, but this time they hadn't been round at all. Better go down to Old Ben's, and ask him."

They went to Old Ben's. No one was at home but "Old Rit," the mother. She said "not one of 'em came dis Christmas. She was looking for 'em all day, an' her heart was mos' broke about 'em."

Old Ben was found and questioned about his sons. Old Ben said, "He hadn't *seen one* of 'em dis Christmas." With all his deep religious feeling, Old Ben thought that in such a case as this, it was enough for him to keep to the *letter,* and let the man hunters find his sons if they could. Old Ben knew the Old Testament stories well. Perhaps he thought of Rahab who hid the spies, and received a commendation for it. Perhaps of Jacob and Abraham, and some of their rather questionable proceedings. He knew the New Testament also, but I think perhaps he thought the kind and loving Saviour would have said to him, "Neither do I condemn thee." I doubt if he had read Mrs. Opie, and I wonder what judgment that excellent woman would have given in a case like this.

These poor fugitives, hunted like partridges upon the mountains, or like the timid fox by the eager sportsman, were obliged in self-defense to meet cunning with cunning, and to borrow from the birds and animals their mode of eluding their pursuers by any device which in the exigency of the case might present itself to them. They had a creed of their own, and a code of morals which we dare not criticise till we find our own lives and those of our dear ones similarly imperiled.

One of Harriet's other brothers had long been attached to a pretty mulatto girl named Catherine, who was owned by another master; but this man had other views for her, and would not let her marry William Henry. On one of Harriet's journeys this brother had made up his mind to make one of her next party to the North, and that Catherine should go also. He went to a tailor's and bought a new suit of clothes for a small person, and concealed them inside the fence of the garden of Catherine's master. This garden ran down to the bank of a little stream, and Catherine had been notified where to find the clothes. When the time came to get ready, Catherine boldly walked down to the foot of the garden, took up the bundle, and hiding under the bank, she put on the man's garments and sent her own floating down the stream.

She was soon missed, and all the girls in the house were set to looking for Catherine. Presently they saw coming up from the river a well-dressed little darkey boy, and they all ceased looking for Catherine, and stared at him. He walked directly by them, round the house, and out of the gate, without the slightest suspicion being excited as to who he was. In a few weeks from that time, this party were all safe in Canada.

William Henry died in Canada, but I have seen and talked with Catherine at Harriet's house.

I am not quite certain which company it was that was under her guidance on their Northward way, but at one time when a number of men were following her, she received one of her sudden intimations that danger was ahead. "Chillen," she said, "we must stop here and cross dis ribber." They were on the bank of a stream of some width, and apparently a deep and rapid one. The men were afraid to cross; there was no bridge and no boat; but like her great pattern, she went forward into the waters, and the men not knowing what else to do, followed, but with fear and trembling. The stream did not divide to make a way for them to cross over, but to her was literally fulfilled the promise:

"When through the deep waters I cause thee to go,
The rivers of sorrow shall not overflow."

"For," said she, "Missus, de water never came above my chin;
when we thought surely we were all going under, it became shallower and shallower, and we came out safe on the odder side."
Then there was another stream to cross, which was also passed
in safety. They found afterward that a few rods ahead of them
the advertisement of these escaping fugitives was posted up,
and the officers, forewarned of their coming, were waiting for
them. But though the Lord thus marvelously protected her from
capture, she did not always escape the consequences of expo-
sure like this. It was in March that this passage of the streams
was effected, and the weather was raw and cold; Harriet traveled a long distance in her wet clothing, and was afterward very
ill for a long time with a very severe cold. I have often heard her
tell this story; but some of the incidents, particularly that of her
illness, were not mentioned by herself, but were written me by
friend Garrett.

I hardly know how to approach the subject of the spiritual
experiences of my sable heroine. They seem so to enter into the
realm of the supernatural, that I can hardly wonder that those
who never knew her are ready to throw discredit upon the story.
Ridicule has been cast upon the whole tale of her adventures by
the advocates of human slavery; and perhaps by those who
would tell with awe-struck countenance some tale of ghostly vis-
itation, or spiritual manifestation, at a dimly lighted *"seance."*

Had I not known so well her deeply religious character, and
her conscientious veracity, and had I not since the war, and
when she was an inmate of my own house, seen such remarkable instances of what seemed to be her direct intercourse with
heaven, I should not dare to risk my own character for veracity
by making these things public in this manner.

But when I add that I have the strongest testimonials to her
character for integrity from William H. Seward, Gerritt Smith,
Wendell Phillips, Fred. Douglass, and my brother, Prof. S. M.
Hopkins, who has known her for many years, I do not fear to
brave the incredulity of any reader.

Governor Seward wrote of her:

"I have known Harriet long, and a nobler, higher spirit, or a truer, seldom dwells in human form."

Gerritt Smith, the distinguished philanthropist, was so kind as to write me expressing his gratification that I had undertaken this work, and added:

"I have often listened to Harriet with delight on her visits to my family, and I am convinced that she is not only truthful, but that she has a rare discernment, and a deep and sublime philanthropy."

Wendell Phillips wrote me, mentioning that in Boston, Harriet earned the confidence and admiration of all those who were working for freedom; and speaking of her labors during the war, he added: "In my opinion there are few captains, perhaps few colonels, who have done more for the loyal cause since the war began, and few men who did more before that time, for the colored race, than our fearless and sagacious friend."

Many other letters I received; from Mr. Sanborn, Secretary of the Massachusetts Board of Charities, from Fred. Douglass, from Rev. Henry Fowler, and from Union officers at the South during the war, all speaking in the highest praise and admiration of the character and labors of my black heroine.

Many of her passes also were sent me; in which she is spoken of as "Moses," for by that name she was universally known. For the story of her heroic deeds had gone before her, and the testimony of all who knew her accorded with the words of Mr. Seward:

"The cause of freedom owes her much; the country owes her much." And yet the country was not willing to pay her anything. Mr. Seward's efforts, seconded by other distinguished men, to get a pension for her, were sneered at in Congress as absurd and quixotic, and the effort failed.

Secretary Seward, from whom Harriet purchased her little place near Auburn, died. The place had been mortgaged when this noble woman left her home, and threw herself into the work needed for the Union cause; the mortgage was to be foreclosed. The old parents, then nearly approaching their centennial year, were to be turned out to die in a poor-house, when the sudden determination was taken to send out a little sketch of her life to the benevolent public, in the hope of redeeming the little home. This object, through the kindness of friends, was accomplished. The old people died in Harriet's own home, breathing blessings upon her for her devotion to them.

Now another necessity has arisen, and our sable friend, who never has been known to beg for herself, asks once more for help in accomplishing a favorite project for the good of her people. This, as she says, is "her last work, and she only prays de Lord to let her live till it is well started, and den she is ready to go." This work is the building of a hospital for old and disabled colored people; and in this she has already had the sympathy and aid of the good people of Auburn; the mayor and his noble wife having given her great assistance in the meetings she has held in aid of this object. It is partly to aid her in this work, on which she has so set her heart, that this story of her life and labors is being re-written.

At one time, when she felt called upon to go down for some company of slaves, she was, as she knew, watched for everywhere (for there had been an excited meeting of slave-holders, and they were determined to catch her, dead or alive), her friends gathered round her, imploring her not to go on in the face of danger and death, for they were sure she would never be allowed to return. And this was her answer:

"Now look yer! John saw de City, didn't he?" "Yes, John saw de City." "Well, what did he see? He saw twelve gates, didn't he? Three of dose gates was on de north; three of 'em was on de east; an' three of 'em was on de west; but dere was three more, an' dem was on de *south;* an' I reckon, if dey kill me down dere, I'll git into one of dem gates, don't you?"

Whether Harriet's ideas of the geographical bearings of the gates of the Celestial City as seen in the apocalyptic vision, were correct or not, we cannot doubt that she was right in the deduction her faith drew from them; and that somewhere, whether North, East, South, or West, to our dim vision, there is a gate that will be opened for our good Harriet, where the welcome will be given, "Come in, thou blessed of my Father."

It is a peculiarity of Harriet, that she had seldom been known to intimate a wish that anything should be given to herself; but when her people are in need, no scruples of delicacy stand in the way of her petitions, nay, almost her *demands* for help.

When, after rescuing so many others, and all of her brothers and sisters that could be reached, with their children, she received an intimation in some mysterious or supernatural way, that the old people were in trouble and needed her, she asked the Lord where she should go for the money to enable her to go for them. She was in some way, as she supposed, directed to the office of a certain gentleman, a friend of the slaves, in New York.

When she left the house of the friends with whom she was staying, she said: "I'm gwine to Mr. ——'s office, an' I ain't gwine to lebe dere, an' I ain't gwine to eat or drink, till I get money enough to take me down after de ole people."

She went into this gentleman's office.

"How do you do, Harriet? What do you want?" was the first greeting.

"I want some money, sir."

"*You do!* How much do you want?"

"I want twenty dollars, sir!"

"*Twenty dollars!* Who told you to come here for twenty dollars!"

"De Lord tole me, sir."

"He did; well I guess the Lord's mistaken this time."

"No, sir; de Lord's nebber mistaken! Anyhow I'm gwine to sit here till I get it."

So she sat down and went to sleep. All the morning, and all the afternoon, she sat there still; sometimes sleeping, sometimes rousing up, often finding the office full of gentlemen; sometimes finding herself alone.

Many fugitives were passing through New York at this time, and those who came in supposed her to be one of them, tired out, and resting. Sometimes she would be roused up with the words:

"Come, Harriet! You had better go; there's no money for you here."

"No, sir; I'm not gwine to stir from here till I git my twenty dollars!"

She does not know all that happened, for deep sleep fell upon her; probably one of the turns of somnolency to which she has always been subject; but without doubt her story was whispered from one to another, and as her name and exploits were well known to many persons, the sympathies of some of those visitors to the office were aroused; at all events she came to full consciousness, at last, to find herself the happy possessor of *sixty dollars*, the contribution of these strangers. She went on her way rejoicing to bring her old parents from the land of bondage.

When she reached their home, she found that her old father was to be tried the next Monday for helping off slaves. And so, as she says in her forcible language, "I just removed my father's trial to a higher court, and brought him off to Canada."

The manner of their escape is detailed in the following letter from friend Garrett:

WILMINGTON, 6th Mo., 1868.

MY FRIEND: Thy favor of the 12th reached me yesterday, requesting such reminiscences as I could give respecting the remarkable labors of Harriet Tubman, in aiding her colored friends from bondage. I may begin by saying, living as I have in a slave State, and the laws being very severe where any proof could be made of any one aiding slaves on their way to freedom, I have not felt at liberty to keep any written word of Harriet's or my own labors, except in numbering those whom I have aided. For that reason I cannot furnish so interesting an account of Harriet's labors as I otherwise could, and now would be glad to do; for in truth I never met with any person, of any color, who had more confidence in the voice of God, as spoken direct to her soul. She has frequently told me that she talked with God, and he talked with her every day of her life, and she has declared to me that she felt no more fear of being arrested by her former master, or any other person, when in his immediate neighborhood, than she did in the State of New York, or Canada, for she said she never ventured only where God sent her, and her faith in the Supreme Power truly was great.

I have now been confined to my room with indisposition more than four weeks, and cannot sit to write much; but I feel so much interested in Harriet, that I will try to give some of the most remarkable incidents that now present themselves to my mind. The date of the commencement of her labors, I cannot certainly give; but I think it must have been about 1845; from that time till 1860, I think she must have brought from the neighborhood where she had been held as a slave from 60 to 80 persons,° from Maryland, some 80 miles from here. No slave who placed himself under her care, was ever arrested that I have heard of; she mostly had her regular stopping places on her route; but in one instance, when she had several stout men with her, some 30 miles below here, she said that God told her to stop, which she did; and then asked him what she must do. He told her to leave the road, and turn to the left; she obeyed, and soon came to a small stream of tide water; there was no boat, no bridge; she again inquired of her Guide what she was to do. She was told to go through. It was cold, in the month of March; but having confidence in her Guide, she went in; the water came up to her armpits; the men refused to follow till they saw her safe on the opposite shore. They then followed, and, if I mistake not, she had soon to wade a second stream; soon after which she came to a cabin of colored people, who took them all in, put them to bed, and dried their clothes, ready to proceed next night on their journey. Harriet had run out of money, and gave them some of her underclothing to pay for their kindness. When she called on me two days after, she was so hoarse she could hardly speak, and was also suffering with violent toothache. The strange part of the story we found to be, that the masters of these men had put up the previous day, at the railroad station near where she left, an advertisement for them, offering a large reward for their apprehension; but they made a safe exit. She at one time brought as many as seven or eight, several of whom were women and children. She was well known here in Chester

---

°Friend Garrett probably refers here to those who passed through his hands. Harriet was obliged to come by many different routes on her different journeys, and though she never counted those whom she brought away with her, it would seem, by the computation of others, that there must have been somewhat over three hundred brought by her to the Northern States and Canada.

County and Philadelphia, and respected by all true abolitionists. I had been in the habit of furnishing her and those who accompanied her, as she returned from her acts of mercy, with new shoes; and on one occasion when I had not seen her for three months, she came into my store. I said, "Harriet, I am glad to see thee! I suppose thee wants a pair of new shoes." Her reply was, "I want more than that." I, in jest, said, "I have always been liberal with thee, and wish to be; but I am not rich, and cannot afford to give much." Her reply was: "God tells me you have money for me." I asked her "if God never deceived her?" She said, "No!" "Well! how much does thee want?" After studying a moment, she said: "About twenty-three dollars." I then gave her twenty-four dollars and some odd cents, the net proceeds of five pounds sterling, received through Eliza Wigham, of Scotland, for her. I had given some accounts of Harriet's labor to the Anti-Slavery Society of Edinburgh, of which Eliza Wigham was Secretary. On the reading of my letter, a gentleman present said he would send Harriet four pounds if he knew of any way to get it to her. Eliza Wigham offered to forward it to me for her, and that was the first money ever received by me for her. Some twelve months after, she called on me again, and said that God told her I had some money for her, but not so much as before. I had, a few days previous, received the net proceeds of one pound ten shillings from Europe for her. To say the least there was something remarkable in these facts, whether clairvoyance, or the divine impression on her mind from the source of all power, I cannot tell; but certain it was she had a guide within herself other than the written word, for she never had any education. She brought away her aged parents in a singular manner. They started with an old horse, fitted out in primitive style with a *straw collar,* a pair of old chaise wheels, with a board on the axle to sit on, another board swung with ropes, fastened to the axle, to rest their feet on. She got her parents, who were both slaves belonging to different masters, on this rude vehicle to the railroad, put them in the cars, turned Jehu herself, and drove to town in a style that no human being ever did before or since; but she was happy at having arrived safe. Next day, I furnished her with money to take them all to Canada. I afterward sold their horse, and sent them the balance of the proceeds. I believe that Harriet succeeded in freeing all her relatives but one sister and her three children. Etc., etc.   Thy friend,

THOS. GARRETT.

As I have before stated, with all Harriet's reluctance to ask for anything for herself, no matter how great her needs may be, no such scruples trouble her if any of her people are in need. She never hesitates to call upon her kind friends in Auburn and in other places for help when her people are in want. At one time, when some such emergency had arisen, she went to see her friend, Governor Seward, and boldly presented her case to him.

"Harriet," he said, "you have worked for others long enough. If you would ever ask anything for yourself, I would gladly give it to you, but I will not help you to rob yourself for others any longer."

In spite of this apparent roughness, we may be sure Harriet did not leave this noble man's house empty handed.

And here I am reminded of a touching little circumstance that occurred at the funeral of Secretary Seward.

The great man lay in his coffin. Friends, children, and admirers were gathered there. Everything that love and wealth could do had been done; around him were floral emblems of every possible shape and design, that human ingenuity could suggest, or money could purchase. Just before the coffin was to be closed, a woman black as night stole quietly in, and laying a wreath of field flowers *on his feet*, as quietly glided out again. This was the simple tribute of our sable friend, and her last token of love and gratitude to her kind benefactor. I think he would have said, "This woman hath done more than ye all."

While preparing this second edition of Harriet's story, I have been much pleased to find that that good man, Oliver Johnson, is still living and in New York City. And I have just returned from a very pleasant interview with him. He remembers Harriet with great pleasure, though he has not seen her for many years. He speaks, as all who knew her do, of his entire confidence in her truthfulness and in the perfect integrity of her character.

He remembered her coming into his office with Joe, as I have stated it, and said he wished he could recall to me other incidents connected with her. But during those years, there were such numbers of fugitive slaves coming into the Anti-Slavery Office, that he might not tell the incidents of any one group correctly. No records were kept, as that would be so unsafe for the poor creatures, and those who aided them. He said, "You know Harriet never spoke of anything she had done, as if it was at all remarkable, or as if it deserved any commendation, but I remember one day, when she came into the office there was a Boston lady there, a warm-hearted, impulsive woman, who was engaged heart and hand in the Anti-Slavery cause.

Harriet was telling, in her simple way, the story of her last journey. A party of fugitives were to meet her in a wood, that she might conduct them North. For some unexplained reason they did not come. Night came on and with it a blinding snow storm and a raging wind. She protected herself behind a tree as well as she could, and remained all night alone exposed to the fury of the storm.

"Why, Harriet!" said this lady, "didn't you almost feel when you were lying alone, as if there was *no God?*" "Oh, no! missus," said Harriet, looking up in her child-like, simple way, "I jest asked Jesus to take keer of me, an' He never let me git *frost-bitten* one bit."

In 1860 the first gun was fired from Fort Sumter; and this was the signal for a rush to arms at the North and the South, and the war of the rebellion was begun. Troops were hurried off from the North to the West and the South, and battles raged in every part of the Southern States. By land and by sea, and on the Southern rivers, the conflict raged, and thousands and thousands of brave men shed their blood for what was maintained by each side to be the true principle.

This war our brave heroine had expected, and its result, the emancipation of the slaves. Three years before, while staying with the Rev. Henry Highland Garnet in New York, a vision came to her in the night of the emancipation of her people. Whether a dream, or one of those glimpses into the future, which sometimes seem to have been granted to her, no one can say, but the effect upon her was very remarkable.

She rose singing, *"My people are free!" "My people are free!"* She came down to breakfast singing the words in a sort of ecstasy. She could not eat. The dream or vision filled her whole soul, and physical needs were forgotten.

Mr. Garnet said to her:

"Oh, Harriet! Harriet! You've come to torment us before the time; do cease this noise! My grandchildren may see the day of the emancipation of our people, but you and I will never see it."

"I tell you, sir, you'll see it, and you'll see it soon. My people are free! My people are free."

When, three years later, President Lincoln's proclamation of emancipation was given forth, and there was a great jubilee among the friends of the slaves, Harriet was continually asked, "Why do you not join with the rest in their rejoicing!" "Oh," she answered, "I had *my* jubilee three years ago. I rejoiced all I could den; I can't rejoice no more."

In some of the Southern States, spies and scouts were needed to lead our armies into the interior. The ignorant and degraded slaves feared the "Yankee Buckra" more than they did their own masters, and after the proclamation of President Lincoln, giving freedom to the slaves, a person in whom these poor creatures could trust, was needed to assure them that these white Northern men were friends, and that they would be safe, trusting themselves in their hands.

In the early days of the war, Governor Andrew of Massachusetts, knowing well the brave and sagacious character of Harriet, sent for her, and asked her if she could go at a moment's notice, to act as spy and scout for our armies, and, if need be, to act as hospital nurse, in short, to be ready to give any required service to the Union cause.

There was much to be thought of; there were the old folks in the little home up in Auburn, there was the little farm of which she had taken the sole care; there were many dependents for whom she had provided by her daily toil. What was to become of them all if she deserted them? But the cause of the Union seemed to need her services, and after a few moments of reflection, she determined to leave all else, and go where it seemed that duty called her.

During those few years, the wants of the old people and of Harriet's other dependents were attended to by the kind people of Auburn. At that time, I often saw the old people, and wrote letters for them to officers at the South, asking from them tidings of Harriet. I received many letters in reply, all testifying to her faithfulness and bravery, and her untiring zeal for the welfare of our soldiers, black and white. She was often under fire from both armies; she led our forces through the jungle and the swamp, guided by an unseen hand. She gained the confidence of the slaves by her cheery words, and songs, and sacred hymns, and obtained from them much valuable information. She nursed our soldiers in the hospitals, and knew how, when they were dying by numbers of some malignant disease, with cunning skill to extract from roots and herbs, which grew near the source of the disease, the healing draught, which allayed the fever and restored numbers to health.

It is a shame to our government that such a valuable helper as this woman was not allowed pay or pension; but even was obliged to support herself during those days of incessant toil. Officers and men were paid. Indeed many enlisted from no patriotic motive, but because they were insured a support which they could not procure for themselves at home. But this woman sacrificed everything, and left her nearest and dearest, and risked her life hundreds of times for the cause of the Union, without one cent of recompense. She returned at last to her little home, to find it a scene of desolation. Her little place about to be sold to satisfy a mortgage, and herself without the means to redeem it.

Harriet was one of John Brown's "men." His brave and daring spirit found ready sympathy in her courageous heart; she sheltered him in her home in Canada, and helped him to plan his campaigns. I find in the life and letters of this remarkable man, written by Mr. F. B. Sanborn, occasional mention of Harriet, and her deep interest in Captain Brown's enterprises.

At one time he writes to his son from St. Catherine's, Canada:
"I came on here the day after you left Rochester. I am succeeding to all appearance beyond my expectations. Harriet Tubman *hooked on her whole team at once*. He (Harriet) is the

most of a man naturally that I ever met with. There is abundant
material here and of the right quality." She suggested the 4th of
July to him as the time to begin operations. And Mr. Sanborn
adds: "It was about the 4th of July, as Harriet, the African sybil,
had suggested, that Brown first showed himself in the counties
of Washington and Jefferson, on opposite sides of the lordly
Potomac."

I find among her papers, many of which are defaced by being
carried about with her for years, portions of these letters
addressed to myself, by persons at the South, and speaking of
the valuable assistance Harriet was rendering our soldiers in the
hospital, and our armies in the field. At this time her manner of
life, as related by herself, was this:

"Well, missus, I'd go to de hospital, I would, early eb'ry
mornin'. I'd get a big chunk of ice, I would, and put it in a basin,
and fill it with water; den I'd take a sponge and begin. Fust man
I'd come to, I'd thrash away de flies, and dey'd rise, dey would,
like bees roun' a hive. Den I'd begin to bathe der wounds, an'
by de time I'd bathed off three or four, de fire and heat would
have melted de ice and made de water warm, an' it would be as
red as clar blood. Den I'd go an' git more ice, I would, an' by de
time I got to de nex' ones, de flies would be roun' de fust ones
black an' thick as eber." In this way she worked, day after day,
till late at night; then she went home to her little cabin, and
made about fifty pies, a great quantity of ginger-bread, and two
casks of root beer. These she would hire some contraband to sell
for her through the camps, and thus she would provide her support for another day; for this woman never received pay or pension, and never drew for herself but twenty days' rations during
the four years of her labors. At one time she was called away
from Hilton Head, by one of our officers, to come to
Fernandina, where the men were "dying off like sheep," from
dysentery. Harriet had acquired quite a reputation for her skill
in curing this disease, by a medicine which she prepared from
roots which grew near the waters which gave the disease. Here
she found thousands of sick soldiers and contrabands, and
immediately gave up her time and attention to them. At another
time, we find her nursing those who were down by hundreds

with small-pox and malignant fevers. She had never had these diseases, but she seems to have no more fear of death in one form than another. "De Lord would take keer of her till her time came, an' den she was ready to go."

When our armies and gun-boats first appeared in any part of the South, many of the poor negroes were as much afraid of "de Yankee Buckra" as of their own masters. It was almost impossible to win their confidence, or to get information from them. But to Harriet they would tell anything; and so it became quite important that she should accompany expeditions going up the rivers, or into unexplored parts of the country, to control and get information from those whom they took with them as guides.

General Hunter asked her at one time if she would go with several gun-boats up the Combahee River, the object of the expedition being to take up the torpedoes placed by the rebels in the river, to destroy railroads and bridges, and to cut off supplies from the rebel troops. She said she would go if Colonel Montgomery was to be appointed commander of the expedition. Colonel Montgomery was one of John Brown's men, and was well known to Harriet. Accordingly, Colonel Montgomery was appointed to the command, and Harriet, with several men under her, the principal of whom was J. Plowden, whose pass I have, accompanied the expedition. Harriet describes in the most graphic manner the appearance of the plantations as they passed up the river; the frightened negroes leaving their work and taking to the woods, at sight of the gun-boats; then coming to peer out like startled deer, and scudding away like the wind at the sound of the steam-whistle. "Well," said one old negro, "Mas'r said de Yankees had horns and tails, but I nebber beliebed it till now." But the word was passed along by the mysterious telegraphic communication existing among these simple people, that these were "Lincoln's gun-boats come to set them free." In vain, then, the drivers used their whips in their efforts to hurry the poor creatures back to their quarters; they all turned and ran for the gun-boats. They came down every road, across every field, just as they had left their work and their cabins; women with children clinging around their necks, hanging to their dresses, running behind, all making at full speed for "Lincoln's gun-boats." Eight hundred poor wretches at one time crowded the banks, with their hands extended toward their deliverers, and they were all taken off upon the gun-boats, and carried down to Beaufort.

"I nebber see such a sight," said Harriet; "we laughed, an' laughed, an' laughed. Here you'd see a woman wid a pail on her head, rice a smokin' in it jus' as she'd taken it from de fire, young one hangin' on behind, one han' roun' her forehead to hold on, 'tother han' diggin' into de rice-pot, eatin' wid all its might; hold of her dress two or three more; down her back a bag wid a pig in it. One woman brought two pigs, a white one an' a black one; we took 'em all on board; named de white pig Beauregard, and de black pig Jeff Davis. Sometimes de women would come wid twins hangin' roun' der necks; 'pears like I nebber see so many twins in my life; bags on der shoulders, baskets on der heads, and young ones taggin' behin', all loaded; pigs squealin', chickens screamin', young ones squallin'." And so they came pouring down to the gun-boats. When they stood on the shore, and the small boats put out to take them off, they all wanted to get in at once. After the boats were crowded, they would hold on to them so that they could not leave the shore. The oarsmen would beat them on their hands, but they would not let go; they were afraid the gun-boats would go off and leave them, and all wanted to make sure of one of these arks of refuge. At length Colonel Montgomery shouted from the upper deck, above the clamor of appealing tones, "Moses, you'll have to give em a song." Then Harriet lifted up her voice, and sang:

> "Of all the whole creation in the East or in the West,
> The glorious Yankee nation is the greatest and the best.
> Come along! Come along! don't be alarmed,
> Uncle Sam is rich enough to give you all a farm."

At the end of every verse, the negroes in their enthusiasm would throw up their hands and shout "Glory," and the row-boats would take that opportunity to push off; and so at last they were all brought on board. The masters fled; houses and barns and railroad bridges were burned, tracks torn up, torpedoes destroyed, and the object of the expedition was fully accomplished.

This fearless woman was often sent into the rebel lines as a spy, and brought back valuable information as to the position of armies and batteries; she has been in battle when the shot was falling like hail, and the bodies of dead and wounded men were dropping around her like leaves in autumn; but the thought of fear never seems to have had place for a moment in her mind. She had her duty to perform, and she expected to be taken care of till it was done.

Would that, instead of taking them in this poor way at second-hand, my readers could hear this woman's graphic accounts of scenes she herself witnessed, could listen to her imitations of negro preachers in their own very peculiar dialect, her singing of camp-meeting hymns, her account of "experience meetings," her imitations of the dances, and the funeral ceremonies of these simple people. "Why, der language down dar in de far South is jus' as different from ours in Maryland as you can tink," said she. "Dey laughed when dey heard me talk, an' I could not understand dem, no how." She described a midnight funeral which she attended; for the slaves, never having been allowed to bury their dead in the day-time, continued the custom of night funerals from habit.

The corpse was laid upon the ground, and the people all sat round, the group being lighted up by pine torches.

The old negro preacher began by giving out a hymn, which was sung by all. "An' oh! I wish you could hear 'em sing, Missus," said Harriet. "Der voices is so sweet, and dey can sing eberyting we sing, an' den dey can sing a great many hymns dat we can't nebber catch at all."

The old preacher began his sermon by pointing to the dead man, who lay in a rude box on the ground before him.

"*Shum?* Ded-a-de-dah! *Shum, David?* Ded-a-de-dah! Now I want you all to *flec'* for moment. Who ob all dis congregation is gwine next to lie ded-e-de-dah? You can't go nowhere's, my frien's and bredren, but Deff 'll fin' you. You can't dig no hole so deep an' bury yourself dar, but God A'mighty's far-seein' eye 'll fin' you, an' Deff 'll come arter you. You can't go into that big fort (pointing to Hilton Head), an' shut yourself up dar; dat fort dat Sesh Buckra said the debil couldn't take, but Deff 'll fin' you

dar. All your frien's may forget you, but Deff 'll nebber forget
you. Now, my bredren, prepare to lie ded-a-de-dah!"

This was the burden of a very long sermon, after which the
whole congregation went round in a sort of solemn dance, called
the "spiritual shuffle," shaking hands with each other, and calling each other by name as they sang:

> "My sis'r Mary's boun' to go;
> My sis'r Nanny's boun' to go;
> My brudder Tony's boun' to go;
> My brudder July's boun' to go."

This to the same tune, till every hand had been shaken by
every one of the company. When they came to Harriet, who was
a stranger, they sang:

> Eberybody's boun' to go!

The body was then placed in a Government wagon, and by
the light of the pine torches, the strange, dark procession moved
along, singing a rude funeral hymn, till they reached the place
of burial.

Harriet's account of her interview with an old negro she met
at Hilton Head, is amusing and interesting. He said, "I'd been
yere seventy-three years, workin' for my master widout even a
dime wages. I'd worked rain-wet sun-dry. I'd worked wid my
mouf full of dust, but could not stop to get a drink of water. I'd
been whipped, an' starved, an' I was always prayin', 'Oh! Lord,
come an' delibber us!' All dat time de birds had been flyin', an'
de rabens had been cryin', and de fish had been swimmin' in de
waters. One day I look up, an' I see a big cloud; it didn't come
up like as de clouds come out far yonder, but it 'peared to be
right ober head. Der was thunders out of dat, an' der was light-
nin's. Den I looked down on de water, an' I see, 'peared to me a
big house in de water, an' out of de big house came great big
eggs, and de good eggs went on trou' de air, an' fell into de fort;
an' de bad eggs burst before dey got dar. Den de Sesh Buckra
begin to run, an' de neber stop running till de git to de swamp,

an' de stick dar an' de die dar. Den I heard 'twas de Yankee ship°
firin' out de big eggs, an dey had come to set us free. Den I
praise de Lord. He come an' put he little finger in de work, an
de Sesh Buckra all go; and de birds stop flyin', and de rabens
stop cryin', an' when I go to catch a fish to eat wid my rice, dey's
no fish dar. De Lord A'mighty 'd come and frightened 'em all
out of de waters. Oh! Praise de Lord! I 'd prayed seventy-three
years, an' now he 's come an' we's all free."

The following account of the subject of this memoir is cut
from the *Boston Commonwealth* of 1863, kindly sent the writer
by Mr. Sanborn:

"It was said long ago that the true romance of America was not
in the fortunes of the Indian, where Cooper sought it, nor in New
England character, where Judd found it, nor in the social contrasts
of Virginia planters, as Thackeray imagined, but in the story of the
fugitive slaves. The observation is as true now as it was before War,
with swift, gigantic hand, sketched the vast shadows, and dashed
in the high lights in which romance loves to lurk and flash forth.
But the stage is enlarged on which these dramas are played, the
whole world now sit as spectators, and the desperation or the mag-
nanimity of a poor black woman has power to shake the nation that
so long was deaf to her cries. We write of one of these heroines, of
whom our slave annals are full—a woman whose career is as extraordinary as the most famous of her sex can show.

"Araminta Ross, now known by her married name of Tubman,
with her sounding Christian name changed to Harriet, is the
grand-daughter of a slave imported from Africa, and has not a
drop of white blood in her veins. Her parents were Benjamin
Ross and Harriet Greene, both slaves, but married and faithful to
each other. They still live in old age and poverty,† but free, on a
little property at Auburn, N. Y., which their daughter purchased
for them from Mr. Seward, the Secretary of State. She was born,
as near as she can remember, in 1820 or in 1821, in Dorchester
County, on the Eastern shore of Maryland, and not far from the

---

°The *Wabash*.
†Both dead for some years.

town of Cambridge. She had ten brothers and sisters, of whom three are now living, all at the North, and all rescued from slavery by Harriet, before the War. She went back just as the South was preparing to secede, to bring away a fourth, but before she could reach her, she was dead. Three years before, she had brought away her old father and mother, at great risk to herself.

"When Harriet was six years old, she was taken from her mother and carried ten miles to live with James Cook, whose wife was a weaver, to learn the trade of weaving. While still a mere child, Cook set her to watching his musk-rat traps, which compelled her to wade through the water. It happened that she was once sent when she was ill with the measles, and, taking cold from wading in the water in this condition, she grew very sick, and her mother persuaded her master to take her away from Cook's until she could get well.

"Another attempt was made to teach her weaving, but she would not learn, for she hated her mistress, and did not want to live at home, as she would have done as a weaver, for it was the custom then to weave the cloth for the family, or a part of it, in the house.

"Soon after she entered her teens she was hired out as a field hand, and it was while thus employed that she received a wound, which nearly proved fatal, from the effects of which she still suffers. In the fall of the year, the slaves there work in the evening, cleaning up wheat, husking corn, etc. On this occasion, one of the slaves of a farmer named Barrett, left his work, and went to the village store in the evening. The overseer followed him, and so did Harriet. When the slave was found, the overseer swore he should be whipped, and called on Harriet, among others, to help tie him. She refused, and as the man ran away, she placed herself in the door to stop pursuit. The overseer caught up a two-pound weight from the counter and threw it at the fugitive, but it fell short and struck Harriet a stunning blow on the head. It was long before she recovered from this, and it has left her subject to a sort of stupor or lethargy at times; coming upon her in the midst of conversation, or whatever she may be doing, and throwing her into a deep slumber, from which she will presently rouse herself, and go on with her conversation or work.

"After this she lived for five or six years with John Stewart, where at first she worked in the house, but afterward 'hired her time,' and Dr. Thompson, son of her master's guardian, 'stood for her,' that is, was her surety for the payment of what she owed. She employed the time thus hired in the rudest labors,—drove oxen, carted, plowed, and did all the work of a man,—sometimes earning money enough in a year, beyond what she paid her master, 'to buy a pair of steers,' worth forty dollars. The amount exacted of a woman for her time was fifty or sixty dollars—of a man, one hundred to one hundred and fifty dollars. Frequently Harriet worked for her father, who was a timber inspector, and superintended the cutting and hauling of great quantities of timber for the Baltimore ship-yards. Stewart, his temporary master, was a builder, and for the work of Ross used to receive as much as five dollars a day sometimes, he being a superior workman. While engaged with her father, she would cut wood, haul logs, etc. Her usual 'stint' was half a cord of wood in a day.

"Harriet was married somewhere about 1844, to a free colored man named John Tubman, but she had no children. For the last two years of slavery she lived with Dr. Thompson, before mentioned, her own master not being yet of age, and Dr. T.'s father being his guardian, as well as the owner of her own father. In 1849 the young man died, and the slaves were to be sold, though previously set free by an old will. Harriet resolved not to be sold, and so, with no knowledge of the North—having only heard of Pennsylvania and New Jersey—she walked away one night alone. She found a friend in a white lady, who knew her story and helped her on her way. After many adventures, she reached Philadelphia, where she found work and earned a small stock of money. With this money in her purse, she traveled back to Maryland for her husband, but she found him married to another woman, and no longer caring to live with her. This, however, was not until two years after her escape, for she does not seem to have reached her old home in the first two expeditions. In December, 1850, she had visited Baltimore and brought away her sister and two children, who had come up from Cambridge in a boat, under charge of her sister's husband,

a free black. A few months after she had brought away her
brother and two other men, but it was not till the fall of 1851,
that she found her husband and learned of his infidelity. She did
not give way to rage or grief, but collected a party of fugitives
and brought them safely to Philadelphia. In December of the
same year, she returned, and led out a party of eleven, among
them her brother and his wife. With these she journeyed to
Canada, and there spent the winter, for this was after the
enforcement of Mason's Fugitive Slave Bill in Philadelphia and
Boston, and there was no safety except 'under the paw of the
British Lion,' as she quaintly said. But the first winter was terri-
bly severe for these poor runaways. They earned their bread by
chopping wood in the snows of a Canadian forest; they were
frost-bitten, hungry, and naked. Harriet was their good angel.
She kept house for her brother, and the poor creatures boarded
with her. She worked for them, begged for them, prayed for
them, with the strange familiarity of communion with God
which seems natural to these people, and carried them by the
help of God through the hard winter.

"In the spring she returned to the States, and as usual earned
money by working in hotels and families as a cook. From Cape
May, in the fall of 1852, she went back once more to Maryland,
and brought away nine more fugitives.

"Up to this time she had expended chiefly her own money in
these expeditions—money which she had earned by hard work
in the drudgery of the kitchen. Never did any one more exactly
fulfill the sense of George Herbert—

"'A servant with this clause
Makes drudgery divine.'

"But it was not possible for such virtues long to remain hidden from the keen eyes of the Abolitionists. She became known
to Thomas Garrett, the large-hearted Quaker of Wilmington,
who has aided the escape of three thousand fugitives; she found
warm friends in Philadelphia and New York, and wherever she
went. These gave her money, which she never spent for her own
use, but laid up for the help of her people, and especially for her

journeys back to the 'land of Egypt,' as she called her old home. By reason of her frequent visits there, always carrying away some of the oppressed, she got among her people the name of 'Moses,' which it seems she still retains.

"Between 1852 and 1857, she made but two of these journeys, in consequence partly of the increased vigilance of the slave-holders, who had suffered so much by the loss of their property. A great reward was offered for her capture and she several times was on the point of being taken, but always escaped by her quick wit, or by 'warnings' from Heaven—for it is time to notice one singular trait in her character. She is the most shrewd and practical person in the world, yet she is a firm believer in omens, dreams, and warnings. She declares that before her escape from slavery, she used to dream of flying over fields and towns, and rivers and mountains, looking down upon them 'like a bird,' and reaching at last a great fence, or sometimes a river, over which she would try to fly, 'but it 'peared like I wouldn't hab de strength, and jes as I was sinkin' down, dere would be ladies all drest in white ober dere, and dey would put out dere arms and pull me 'cross.' There is nothing strange in this, perhaps, but she declares that when she came North she remembered these very places as those she had seen in her dreams, and many of the ladies who befriended her were those she had been helped by in her vision.

"Then she says she always knows when there is danger near her—she does not know how, exactly, but ''pears like my heart go flutter, flutter, and den dey may say "Peace, Peace," as much as dey likes, *I know its gwine to be war!*' She is very firm on this point, and ascribes to this her great impunity, in spite of the lethargy before mentioned, which would seem likely to throw her into the hands of her enemies. She says she inherited this power, that her father could always predict the weather, and that he foretold the Mexican war.

"In 1857 she made her most venturesome journey, for she brought with her to the North her old parents, who were no longer able to walk such distances as she must go by night. Consequently she must hire a wagon for them, and it required all her ingenuity to get them through Maryland and Delaware safe. She accomplished it, however, and by the aid of her friends she brought them safe to Canada, where they spent the winter. Her account of their sufferings there—of her mother's complaining and her own philosophy about it—is a lesson of trust in Providence better than many sermons. But she decided to bring them to a more comfortable place, and so she negotiated with Mr. Seward—then in the Senate—for a little patch of ground. To the credit of the Secretary of State it should be said, that he sold her the property on very favorable terms, and gave her some time for payment. To this house she removed her parents, and set herself to work to pay for the purchase. It was on this errand that she first visited Boston—we believe in the winter of 1858–59. She brought a few letters from her friends in New York, but she could herself neither read nor write, and she was obliged to trust to her wits that they were delivered to the right persons. One of them, as it happened, was to the present writer, who received it by another hand, and called to see her at her boarding-house. It was curious to see the caution with which she received her visitor until she felt assured that there was no mistake. One of her means of security was to carry with her the daguerreotypes of her friends, and show them to each new person. If they recognized the likeness, then it was all right.

"Pains were taken to secure her the attention to which her great services of humanity entitled her, and she left New England with a handsome sum of money toward the payment of her debt to Mr. Seward. Before she left, however, she had several interviews with Captain Brown, then in Boston. He is supposed to have communicated his plans to her, and to have been aided by her in obtaining recruits and money among her people. At any rate, he always spoke of her with the greatest respect, and declared that 'General Tubman,' as he styled her, was a better officer than most whom he had seen, and could command an army as successfully as she had led her small parties of fugitives.

"Her own veneration for Captain Brown has always been profound, and since his murder, has taken the form of a religion. She had often risked her own life for her people, and she thought nothing of that; but that a white man, and a man so noble and strong, should so take upon himself the burden of a despised race, she could not understand, and she took refuge from her perplexity in the mysteries of her fervid religion.

"Again, she laid great stress on a dream which she had just before she met Captain Brown in Canada. She thought she was in 'a wilderness sort of place, all full of rocks, and bushes,' when she saw a serpent raise its head among the rocks, and as it did so, it became the head of an old man with a long white beard, gazing at her, 'wishful like, jes as ef he war gwine to speak to me,' and then two other heads rose up beside him, younger than he,—and as she stood looking at them, and wondering what they could want with her, a great crowd of men rushed in and struck down the younger heads, and then the head of the old man, still looking at her so 'wishful.' This dream she had again and again, and could not interpret it; but when she met Captain Brown, shortly after, behold, he was the very image of the head she had seen. But still she could not make out what her dream signified, till the news came to her of the tragedy of Harper's Ferry, and then she knew the two other heads were his two sons. She was in New York at that time, and on the day of the affair at Harper's Ferry she felt her usual warning that something was wrong— she could not tell what. Finally she told her hostess that it must be Captain Brown who was in trouble, and that they should soon hear bad news from him. The next day's newspaper brought tidings of what had happened.

"Her last visit to Maryland was made after this, in December, 1860; and in spite of the agitated condition of the country, and the greater watchfulness of the slave-holders, she brought away seven fugitives, one of them an infant, which must be drugged with opium to keep it from crying on the way, and so revealing the hiding-place of the party."

In the spring of 1860, Harriet Tubman was requested by Mr. Gerrit Smith to go to Boston to attend a large Anti-Slavery meeting. On her way, she stopped at Troy to visit a cousin, and while there the colored people were one day startled with the intelligence that a fugitive slave, by the name of Charles Nalle, had been followed by his master (who was his younger brother, and not one grain whiter than he), and that he was already in the hands of the officers, and was to be taken back to the

South. The instant Harriet heard the news, she started for the office of the United States Commissioner, scattering the tidings as she went. An excited crowd was gathered about the office, through which Harriet forced her way, and rushed up stairs to the door of the room where the fugitive was detained. A wagon was already waiting before the door to carry off the man, but the crowd was even then so great, and in such a state of excitement, that the officers did not dare to bring the man down. On the opposite side of the street stood the colored people, watching the window where they could see Harriet's sun-bonnet, and feeling assured that so long as she stood there, the fugitive was still in the office. Time passed on, and he did not appear. "They've taken him out another way, depend upon that," said some of the colored people. "No," replied others, "there stands 'Moses' yet, and as long as she is there, he is safe." Harriet, now seeing the necessity for a tremendous effort for his rescue, sent out some little boys to cry *fire*. The bells rang, the crowd increased, till the whole street was a dense mass of people. Again and again the officers came out to try and clear the stairs, and make a way to take their captive down; others were driven down, but Harriet stood her ground, her head bent and her arms folded. "Come, old woman, you must get out of this," said one of the officers; "I must have the way cleared; if you can't get down alone, some one will help you." Harriet, still putting on a greater appearance of decrepitude, twitched away from him, and kept her place. Offers were made to buy Charles from his master, who at first agreed to take twelve hundred dollars for him; but when this was subscribed, he immediately raised the price to fifteen hundred. The crowd grew more excited. A gentleman raised a window and called out, "Two hundred dollars for his rescue, but not one cent to his master!" This was responded to by a roar of satisfaction from the crowd below. At length the officers appeared, and announced to the crowd, that if they would open a lane to the wagon, they would promise to bring the man down the front way.

The lane was opened, and the man was brought out—a tall, handsome, intelligent *white* man, with his wrists manacled together, walking between the U.S. Marshal and another officer, and behind him his brother and his master, so like him that one could hardly be told from the other. The moment they appeared, Harriet roused from her stooping posture, threw up a window, and cried to her friends: "Here he comes—take him!" and then darted down the stairs like a wild-cat. She seized one officer and pulled him down, then another, and tore him away from the man; and keeping her arms about the slave, she cried to her friends: "Drag us out! Drag him to the river! Drown him! but don't let them have him!" They were knocked down together, and while down, she tore off her sun-bonnet and tied it on the head of the fugitive. When he rose, only his head could be seen, and amid the surging mass of people the slave was no longer recognized, while the master appeared like the slave. Again and again they were knocked down, the poor slave utterly helpless, with his manacled wrists, streaming with blood. Harriet's outer clothes were torn from her, and even her stout shoes were pulled from her feet, yet she never relinquished her hold of the man, till she had dragged him to the river, where he was tumbled into a boat, Harriet following in a ferry-boat to the other side. But the telegraph was ahead of them, and as soon as they landed he was seized and hurried from her sight. After a time, some school children came hurrying along, and to her anxious inquiries they answered, "He is up in that house, in the third story." Harriet rushed up to the place. Some men were attempting to make their way up the stairs. The officers were firing down, and two men were lying on the stairs, who had been shot. Over their bodies our heroine rushed, and with the help of others burst open the door of the room, and dragged out the fugitive, whom Harriet carried down stairs in her arms. A gentleman who was riding by with a fine horse, stopped to ask what the disturbance meant; and on hearing the story, his sympathies seemed to be thoroughly aroused; he sprang from his wagon, calling out, "That is a blood-horse, drive him till he drops." The poor man was hurried in; some of his friends jumped in after him and drove at the most rapid rate to Schenectady.

This is the story Harriet told to the writer. By some persons it seemed too wonderful for belief, and an attempt was made to corroborate it. Rev. Henry Fowler, who was at the time at Saratoga, kindly volunteered to go to Troy and ascertain the facts. His report was, that he had had a long interview with Mr. Townsend, who acted during the trial as counsel for the slave, that he had given him a "rich narration," which he would write out the next week for this little book. But before he was to begin his generous labor, and while engaged in some kind efforts for the prisoners at Auburn, he was stricken down by the heat of the sun, and was for a long time debarred from labor.

This good man died not long after and the promised narration was never written, but a statement by Mr. Townsend was sent me, which I copy here:

Statements made by Martin I. Townsend, Esq., of Troy, who was counsel for the fugitive, Charles Nalle.

Nalle is an octoroon; his wife has the same infusion of Caucasian blood. She was the daughter of her master, and had, with her sister, been bred by him in his family, as his own child. When the father died, both of these daughters were married and had large families of children. Under the highly Christian national laws of "Old Virginny," these children were the slaves of their grandfather. The old man died, leaving a will, whereby he manumitted his daughters and their children, and provided for the purchase of the freedom of their husbands. The manumission of the children and grandchildren took effect; but the estate was insufficient to purchase the husbands of his daughters, and the fathers of his grandchildren. The manumitted, by another Christian, "conservative," and "national" provision of law, were forced to leave the State, while the slave husbands remained in slavery. Nalle, and his brother-in-law, were allowed for a while to visit their families outside Virginia about once a year, but were at length ordered to provide themselves with new wives, as they would be allowed to visit their former ones no more. It was after this that Nalle and his brother-in-law started for the land of freedom, guided by the steady light of the north star. Thank God, neither family now need fear any earthly master or the bay of the blood-hound dogging their fugitive steps.

Nalle returned to Troy with his family about July, 1860, and resided with them there for more than seven years. They are all now residents of the city of Washington, D. C. Nalle and his family are persons of refined manners, and of the highest respectability. Several of his children are red-haired, and a stranger would discover no trace of African blood in their complexions or features. It was the head of this family whom H. F. Averill proposed to doom to returnless exile and life-long slavery.

When Nalle was brought from Commissioner Beach's office into the street, Harriet Tubman, who had been standing with the excited crowd, rushed amongst the foremost to Nalle, and running one of her arms around his manacled arm, held on to him without ever loosening her hold through the more than half-hour's struggle to Judge Gould's office, and from Judge Gould's office to the dock, where Nalle's liberation was accomplished. In the *mêlée* she was repeatedly beaten over the head with policemen's clubs, but she never for a moment released her hold, but cheered Nalle and his friends with her voice, and struggled with the officers until they were literally worn out with their exertions, and Nalle was separated from them.

True, she had strong and earnest helpers in her struggle, some of whom had white faces as well as human hearts, and are now in Heaven. But she exposed herself to the fury of the sympathizers with slavery, without fear, and suffered their blows without flinching. Harriet crossed the river with the crowd, in the ferry-boat, and when the men who led the assault upon the door of Judge Stewart's office were stricken down, Harriet and a number of other colored women rushed over their bodies, brought Nalle out, and putting him in the first wagon passing, started him for the West.

A lively team, driven by a colored man, was immediately sent on to relieve the other, and Nalle was seen about Troy no more until he returned a free man by purchase from his master. Harriet also disappeared, and the crowd dispersed. How she came to be in Troy that day, is entirely unknown to our citizens; and where she hid herself after the rescue, is equally a mystery. But her struggle was in the sight of a thousand, perhaps of five thousand spectators.

On asking Harriet particularly, as to the age of her mother, she answered, "Well, I'll tell you, Missus. Twenty-three years ago, in Maryland, I paid a lawyer five dollars to look up the will of my mother's first master. He looked back sixty years, and said it was time to give up. I told him to go back furder. He went back sixty-five years, and there he found the will—giving the girl Ritty to his grand-daughter (Mary Patterson), to serve her and her offspring till she was forty-five years of age." This grand-daughter died soon after, unmarried; and as there was no provision for Ritty, in case of her death, she was actually emancipated at that time. But no one informed her of the fact, and she and her dear children remained in bondage till emancipated by the courage and determination of this heroic daughter and sister. The old woman must then, it seems, be ninety-eight years of age,* and the old man has probably numbered as many years. And yet these old people, living out beyond the toll-gate, on the South Street road, Auburn, come in every Sunday—more than a mile—to the Central Church. To be sure, deep slumbers settle down upon them as soon as they are seated, which continue undisturbed till the congregation is dismissed; but they have done their best, and who can doubt that they receive a blessing. Immediately after this they go to class-meeting at the Methodist Church. Then they wait for a third service, and after that start out home again.

Harriet supposes that the whole family were actually free, and were kept wrongfully in a state of slavery all those long years; but she simply states the fact, without any mourning or lamenting over the wrong and the misery of it all, accepting it as the will of God, and, therefore, not to be rebelled against.

This woman, of whom you have been reading, is now old and feeble, suffering from the effects of her life of unusual labor and hardship, as well as from repeated injuries; but she is still at work for her people. For many years, even long before the war, her little home has been the refuge of the

---

*This was written in the year '68, and the old people both lived several years after that time.

hunted and the homeless, for whom she had provided; and I have seen as many as eight or ten dependents upon her care at one time living there.

It has always been a hospital, but she feels the need of a large one, and only prays to see this, "her last work," completed ere she goes hence.

Without claiming any of my dear old Harriet's prophetic vision, I seem to see a future day when the wrongs of earth will be righted, and justice, long delayed, will assert itself. I seem to see that our poor Harriet has passed within "one of dem gates," and has received the welcome, "Come, thou blessed of my Father; for I was hungry and you gave me meat, I was thirsty and you gave me drink, I was a stranger and you took me in, naked and you clothed me, sick and in prison and you visited me."

And when she asks, "Lord, when did I do all this?" He answers: "Inasmuch as you did it unto one of the least of these, *my brethren,* you did it unto me."

And as she stands in her modest way just within the celestial gate, I seem to see a kind hand laid upon her dark head, and to hear a gentle voice saying in her ear, "Friend, come up higher!"

APPENDIX

THE following letters to the writer from those well-known and distinguished philanthropists, Hon. Gerrit Smith and Wendell Phillips, and one from Frederick Douglass, addressed to Harriet, will serve as the best introduction that can be given of the subject of this memoir to its readers:

Letter from Hon. Gerrit Smith.

PETERBORO, *June* 13, 1868.

MY DEAR MADAME: I am happy to learn that you are to speak to the public of Mrs. Harriet Tubman. Of the remarkable events of her life I have no *personal* knowledge, but of the truth of them as she describes them I have no doubt.

I have often listened to her, in her visits to my family, and I am confident that she is not only truthful, but that she has a rare discernment, and a deep and sublime philanthropy.

With great respect your friend,

GERRIT SMITH.

Letter from Wendell Phillips.

June 16, 1868.

DEAR MADAME: The last time I ever saw John Brown was under my own roof, as he brought Harriet Tubman to me, saying: "Mr. Phillips, I bring you one of the best and bravest persons on this continent—*General* Tubman, as we call her."

He then went on to recount her labors and sacrifices in behalf of her race. After that, Harriet spent some time in Boston, earning the confidence and admiration of all those who were working for freedom. With their aid she went to the South more than once, returning always with a squad of self-emancipated men, women, and children, for whom her marvelous skill had opened the way of escape. After the war broke out, she was sent with indorsements from Governor Andrew and his friends to South Carolina, where in the service of the Nation she rendered most important and efficient aid to our army.

In my opinion there are few captains, perhaps few colonels, who have done more for the loyal cause since the war began, and few men who did before that time more for the colored race, than our fearless and most sagacious friend, Harriet.

Faithfully yours,

Wendell Phillips.

Letter from Frederick Douglass.

ROCHESTER, August 29, 1868.

DEAR HARRIET: I am glad to know that the story of your eventful life has been written by a kind lady, and that the same is soon to be published. You ask for what you do not need when you call upon me for a word of commendation. I need such words from you far more than you can need them from me, especially where your superior labors and devotion to the cause of the lately enslaved of our land are known as I know them. The difference between us is very marked. Most that I have done and suffered in the service of our cause has been in public, and I have received much encouragement at every step of the way. You, on the other hand, have labored in a private way. I have wrought in the day—you in the night. I have had the applause of the crowd and the satisfaction that comes of being approved by the multitude, while the most that you have done has been witnessed by a few trembling, scarred, and foot-sore bondmen and women, whom you have led out of the house of bondage, and whose heartfelt *"God bless you"* has been your only reward. The midnight sky and the silent stars have been the witnesses of your devotion to freedom and of your heroism. Excepting John Brown—of sacred

memory—I know of no one who has willingly encountered
more perils and hardships to serve our enslaved people
than you have. Much that you have done would seem
improbable to those who do not know you as I know you.
It is to me a great pleasure and a great privilege to bear testimony to your character and your works, and to say to
those to whom you may come, that I regard you in every
way truthful and trustworthy.

Your friend, ·

FREDERICK DOUGLASS.

---

*Extracts from a Letter written by Mr. Sanborn, Secretary
of the Massachusetts Board of State Charities.*

MY DEAR MADAME: Mr. Phillips has sent me your note,
asking for reminiscences of Harriet Tubman, and testimonials to her extraordinary story, which all her New England
friends will, I am sure, be glad to furnish.

I never had reason to doubt the truth of what Harriet
said in regard to her own career, for I found her singularly
truthful. Her imagination is warm and rich, and there is a
whole region of the marvelous in her nature, which has
manifested itself at times remarkably. Her dreams and
visions, misgivings and forewarnings, ought not to be omitted in any life of her, particularly those relating to John
Brown.

She was in his confidence in 1858–9, and he had a great
regard for her, which he often expressed to me. She aided
him in his plans, and expected to do so still further, when
his career was closed by that wonderful campaign in
Virginia. The first time she came to my house, in Concord,
after that tragedy, she was shown into a room in the
evening, where Brackett's bust of John Brown was standing. The sight of it, which was new to her, threw her into a
sort of ecstacy of sorrow and admiration, and she went on
in her rhapsodical way to pronounce his apotheosis.

She has often been in Concord, where she resided at
the houses of Emerson, Alcott, the Whitneys, the Brooks

family, Mrs. Horace Mann, and other well-known persons.
They all admired and respected her, and nobody doubted
the reality of her adventures. She was too *real* a person to
be suspected. In 1862, I think it was, she went from
Boston to Port Royal, under the advice and encouragement of Mr. Garrison, Governor Andrew, Dr. Howe, and
other leading people. Her career in South Carolina is
well known to some of our officers, and I think to Colonel
Higginson, now of Newport, R. I., and Colonel James
Montgomery, of Kansas, to both of whom she was useful
as a spy and guide, if I mistake not. I regard her as, on the
whole, the most extraordinary person of her race I have
ever met. She is a negro of pure, or almost pure blood,
can neither read nor write, and has the characteristics of
her race and condition. But she has done what can
scarcely be credited on the best authority, and she has
accomplished her purposes with a coolness, foresight,
patience and wisdom, which in a *white man* would have
raised him to the highest pitch of reputation.

I am, dear Madame, very truly your servant,

F. B. SANBORN.

Letter from Hon. Wm. H. Seward.

WASHINGTON, *July* 25, 1868.

MAJ.-GEN. HUNTER—

MY DEAR SIR: Harriet Tubman, a colored woman, has
been nursing our soldiers during nearly all the war. She
believes she has a claim for faithful services to the command in South Carolina with which you are connected,
and she thinks that you would be disposed to see her claim
justly settled.

I have known her long, and a nobler, higher spirit, or a
truer, seldom dwells in the human form. I commend her,
therefore, to your kind and best attentions.

Faithfully your friend,

WILLIAM H. SEWARD.

Letter from Col. James Montgomery.
ST. HELENA ISLAND, S. C., *July* 6, 1863.
HEADQUARTERS COLORED BRIGADE.

BRIG.-GEN. GILMORE, Commanding Department of the South—

GENERAL: I wish to commend to your attention, Mrs. Harriet Tubman, a most remarkable woman, and invaluable as a scout. I have been acquainted with her character and actions for several years.

I am, General, your most ob't servant,

JAMES MONTGOMERY, Col. Com. Brigade.

———

Letter from Mrs. Gen. A. Baird.
PETERBORO, *Nov.* 24, 1864.

The bearer of this, Harriet Tubman, a most excellent woman, who has rendered faithful and good services to our Union army, not only in the hospital, but in various capacities, having been employed under Government at Hilton Head, and in Florida; and I commend her to the protection of all officers in whose department she may happen to be.

She has been known and esteemed for years by the family of my uncle, Hon. Gerrit Smith, as a person of great rectitude and capabilities.

MRS. GEN. A. BAIRD.

———

Letter from Hon. Gerrit Smith.
PETERBORO , N. Y., *Nov.* 4, 1867.

I have known Mrs. Harriet Tubman for many years. Seldom, if ever, have I met with a person more philanthropic, more self-denying, and of more bravery. Nor must I omit to say that she combines with her sublime spirit, remarkable discernment and judgment.

During the late war, Mrs. Tubman was eminently faithful and useful to the cause of our country. She is poor and has poor parents. Such a servant of the country should be well paid by the country. I hope that the Government will look into her case.

GERRIT SMITH.

Testimonial from Gerrit Smith.

PETERBORO , Nov. 22, 1864.

The bearer, Harriet Tubman, needs not any recommendation. Nearly all the nation over, she has been heard of for her wisdom, integrity, patriotism, and bravery. The cause of freedom owes her much. The country owes her much.

I have known Harriet for many years, and I hold her in my high esteem.

GERRIT SMITH.

Certificate from Henry K. Durrant,
Acting Asst. Surgeon, U. S. A.

I certify that I have been acquainted with Harriet Tubman for nearly two years; and my position as Medical Officer in charge of "contrabands" in this town and in hospital, has given me frequent and ample opportunities to observe her general deportment; particularly her kindness and attention to the sick and suffering of her own race. I take much pleasure in testifying to the esteem in which she is generally held.

HENRY K. DURRANT,
Acting Assistant Surgeon, U. S. A.
In charge "Contraband" Hospital.

Dated at Beaufort, S. C., the 3d day of May, 1864.

I concur fully in the above.

R. SAXTON, Brig.-Gen. Vol.

The following are a few of the passes used by Harriet throughout the war. Many others are so defaced that it is impossible to decipher them.

HEADQUARTERS DEPARTMENT OF THE SOUTH,
HILTON HEAD, PORT ROYAL, S. C., *Feb.* 19, 1863.

Pass the bearer, Harriet Tubman, to Beaufort and back to this place, and wherever she wishes to go; and give her free passage at all times, on all Government transports. Harriet was sent to me from Boston by Governor Andrew, of Massachusetts, and is a valuable woman. She has permission, as a servant of the Government, to purchase such provisions from the Commissary as she may need.

D. HUNTER, Maj.-Gen. Com.

General Gilmore, who succeeded General Hunter in command of the Department of the South, appends his signature to the same pass.

HEADQUARTERS OF THE DEPARTMENT OF THE SOUTH,
July 1, 1863.
Continued in force.

Q. A. GILMORE, Brig.-Gen. Com.

BEAUFORT, *Aug.* 28, 1862.
Will Capt. Warfield please let "Moses" have a little Bourbon whiskey for medicinal purposes.

HENRY K. DURRANT, Act. Ass. Surgeon.

WAR DEPARTMENT, WASHINGTON, D. C.,
March 20, 1865.
Pass Mrs. Harriet Tubman (colored) to Hilton Head and Charleston, S.C., with free transportation on a Government transport,

By order of the Sec. of War.

LOUIS H., Asst. Adj.-Gen., U. S. A.

To Bvt. Brig.-Gen. Van Vliet, U. S. Q. M., N. Y.
Not transferable.

WAR DEPARTMENT, WASHINGTON, D. C.,
July 22, 1865.

Permit Harriet Tubman to proceed to Fortress Monroe, Va., on a Government transport. Transportation will be furnished free of cost.

By order of the Secretary of War.

L. H., Asst. Adj.-Gen.

Not transferable.

Appointment as Nurse.

SIR: I have the honor to inform you that the Medical Director Department of Virginia has been instructed to appoint Harriet Tubman nurse or matron at the Colored Hospital, Fort Monroe, Va.

Very respectfully, your obdt. servant,

V. K. BARNES, Surgeon-General.

Hon. WM. H. SEWARD,

Secretary of State, Washington, D.C.

Of the many letters, testimonials, and passes, placed in the hands of the writer by Harriet, the following are selected for insertion in this book, and are quite sufficient to verify her statements.

A Letter from Gen. Saxton to a lady of Auburn.

ATLANTA, GA., *March* 21, 1868.

MY DEAR MADAME: I have just received your letter informing me that Hon. W. H. Seward, Secretary of State, would present a petition to Congress for a pension to Harriet Tubman, for services rendered in the Union Army during the late war. I can bear witness to the value of her services in South Carolina and Florida. She was employed in the hospitals and as a spy. She made many a raid inside the enemy's lines, displaying remarkable courage, zeal, and fidelity. She was employed by General Hunter, and I think by Generals Stevens and Sherman, and is as deserving of a pension from the Government for her services as any other of its faithful servants.

I am very truly yours,

RUFUS SAXTON, Bvt. Brig.-Gen., U. S. A.

Rev. Samuel I. May, in his recollections of the anti-slavery conflict, after mentioning the case of an old slave mother, whom he vainly endeavored to assist her son in buying from her master, says:

"I did not until four years after know that remarkable woman Harriet, or I might have engaged her services, in the assurance that she would have bought off the old woman without *paying* for her inalienable right—her liberty."

Mr. May in another place says of Harriet, that she deserves to be placed *first* on the list of American heroines, and then proceeds to give a short account of her labors, varying very little from that given in this book.

FUGITIVE SLAVE RESCUE IN TROY.

From the *Troy Whig*, April 28, 1859.

Yesterday afternoon, the streets of this city and West Troy were made the scenes of unexampled excitement. For the first time since the passage of the Fugitive Slave Law, an attempt was made here to carry its provisions into execution, and the result was a terrific encounter between the officers and the prisoner's friends, the triumph of mob law, and the final rescue of the fugitive. Our city was thrown into a grand state of turmoil, and for a time every other topic was forgotten, to give place to this new excitement. People did not think last evening to ask who was nominated at Charleston, or whether the news of the Heenan and Sayers battle had arrived—everything was merged into the fugitive slave case, of which it seems the end is not yet.

Charles Nalle, the fugitive, who was the cause of all this excitement, was a slave on the plantation of B. W. Hansborough, in Culpepper County, Virginia, till the 19th of October, 1858, when he made his escape, and went to live in Columbia, Pennsylvania. A wife and five children are residing there now. Not long since he came to Sandlake, in this county, and resided in the family of Mr. Crosby until about three weeks ago. Since that time, he has been employed as coachman by Uri Gilbert, Esq., of this city.

He is about thirty years of age, tall, quite light-complex-
ioned, and good-looking. He is said to have been an excellent and faithful servant.

At Sandlake, we understand that Nalle was often seen
by one H. F. Averill, formerly connected with one of the
papers of this city, who communicated with his reputed
owner in Virginia, and gave the information that led to a
knowledge of the whereabouts of the fugitive. Averill
wrote letters for him, and thus obtained an acquaintance
with his history. Mr. Hansborough sent on an agent, Henry
J. Wall, by whom the necessary papers were got out to
arrest the fugitive.

Yesterday morning about 11 o'clock, Charles Nalle was
sent to procure some bread for the family by whom he
was employed. He failed to return. At the baker's he was
arrested by Deputy United States Marshal J. W. Holmes,
and immediately taken before United States Commissioner
Miles Beach. The son of Mr. Gilbert, thinking it strange
that he did not come back, sent to the house of William
Henry, on Division Street, where he boarded, and his
whereabouts was discovered.

The examination before Commissioner Beach was quite
brief. The evidence of Averill and the agent was taken, and
the Commissioner decided to remand Nalle to Virginia.
The necessary papers were made out and given to the
Marshal.

By this time it was two o'clock, and the fact began to be
noised abroad that there was a fugitive slave in Mr.
Beach's office, corner of State and First Streets. People in
knots of ten or twelve collected near the entrance, looking at Nalle, who could be seen at an upper window.
William Henry, a colored man, with whom Nalle
boarded, commenced talking from the curb-stone in a
loud voice to the crowd. He uttered such sentences as,
"There is a fugitive slave in that office—pretty soon you
will see him come forth. He is going to be taken down
South, and you will have a chance to see him. He is to be
taken to the depot, to go to Virginia in the first train.

Keep watch of those stairs, and you will have a sight." A number of women kept shouting, crying, and by loud appeals excited the colored persons assembled.

Still the crowd grew in numbers. Wagons halted in front of the locality, and were soon piled with spectators. An alarm of fire was sounded, and hose carriages dashed through the ranks of men, women, and boys; but they closed again, and kept looking with expectant eyes at the window where the negro was visible. Meanwhile, angry discussions commenced. Some persons agitated a rescue, and others favored law and order. Mr. Brockway, a lawyer, had his coat torn for expressing his sentiments, and other *mêlées* kept the interest alive.

All at once there was a wild halloo, and every eye was turned up to see the legs and part of the body of the prisoner protruding from the second story window, at which he was endeavoring to escape. Then arose a shout! "Drop him!" "Catch him!" "Hurrah!" But the attempt was a fruitless one, for somebody in the office pulled Nalle back again, amid the shouts of a hundred pairs of lungs. The crowd at this time numbered nearly a thousand persons. Many of them were black, and a good share were of the female sex. They blocked up State Street from First Street to the alley, and kept surging to and fro.

Martin I. Townsend, Esq., who acted as counsel for the fugitive, did not arrive in the Commissioner's office until a decision had been rendered. He immediately went before Judge Gould, of the Supreme Court, and procured a writ of habeas corpus in the usual form, *returnable* immediately. This was given Deputy-Sheriff Nathaniel Upham, who at once proceeded to Commissioner Beach's office, and served it on Holmes. Very injudiciously, the officers proceeded at once to Judge Gould's office, although it was evident they would have to pass through an excited, unreasonable crowd. As soon as the officers and their prisoner emerged from the door, an old negro, who had been standing at the bottom of the stairs, shouted, "Here they come," and the crowd made a terrific rush at the party.

From the office of Commissioner Beach, in the Mutual
Building, to that of Judge Gould, in Congress Street, is less
than two blocks, but it was made a regular battlefield. The
moment the prisoner emerged from the doorway, in
custody of Deputy-Sheriff Upham, Chief of Police Quin,
Officers Cleveland and Holmes, the crowd made one
grand charge, and those nearest the prisoner seized him
violently, with the intention of pulling him away from the
officers, but they were foiled; and down First to Congress
Street, and up the latter in front of Judge Gould's cham-
bers, went the surging mass. Exactly what did go on in the
crowd, it is impossible to say, but the pulling, hauling,
mauling, and shouting, gave evidences of frantic efforts on
the part of the rescuers, and a stern resistance from the
conservators of the law. In front of Judge Gould's office the
combat was at its height. No stones or other missiles were
used; the battle was fist to fist. We believe an order was
given to take the prisoner the other way, and there was a
grand rush towards the West, past First and River Streets,
as far as Dock Street. All this time there was a continual
mêlée. Many of the officers were hurt—among them Mr.
Upham, whose object was solely to do his duty by taking
Nalle before Judge Gould in accordance with the writ of
habeas corpus. A number in the crowd were more or less
hurt, and it is a wonder that these were not badly injured,
as pistols were drawn and chisels used.

The battle had raged as far as the corner of Dock and
Congress Streets, and the victory remained with the rescuers at last. The officers were completely worn out with
their exertions, and it was impossible to continue their
hold upon him any longer. Nalle was at liberty. His friends
rushed him down Dock Street to the lower ferry, where
there was a skiff lying ready to start. The fugitive was put
in, the ferryman rowed off, and amid the shouts of hundreds who lined the banks of the river, Nalle was carried
into Albany County.

As the skiff landed in West Troy, a negro sympathizer
waded up to the waist, and pulled Nalle out of the boat. He

went up the hill alone, however, and there who should he meet but Constable Becker! The latter official seeing a man with manacles on, considered it his duty to arrest him. He did so, and took him in a wagon to the office of Justice Stewart, on the second floor of the corner building near the ferry. The justice was absent.

When the crowd on the Troy bank had seen Nalle safely landed, it was suggested that he might be recaptured. Then there was another rush made for the steam ferryboat, which carried over about 400 persons, and left as many more—a few of the latter being soused in their efforts to get on the boat. On landing in West Troy, there, sure enough, was the prisoner, locked up in a strong office, protected by Officers Becker, Brown and Morrison, and the door barricaded.

Not a moment was lost. Up stairs went a score or more of resolute men—the rest "piling in" promiscuously, shouting and execrating the officers. Soon a stone flew against the door—then another—and bang, bang! went off a couple of pistols, but the officers who fired them took good care to aim pretty high. The assailants were forced to retreat for a moment. "They've got pistols," said one. "Who cares?" was the reply; "they can only kill a dozen of us—come on." More stones and more pistol-shots ensued. At last the door was pulled open by an immense negro, and in a moment he was felled by a hatchet in the hands of Deputy-Sheriff Morrison; but the body of the fallen man blocked up the door so that it could not be shut, and a friend of the prisoner pulled him out. Poor fellow! he might well say, "Save me from my friends." Amid the pulling and hauling, the iron had cut his arms, which were bleeding profusely, and he could hardly walk, owing to fatigue.

He has since arrived safely in Canada.

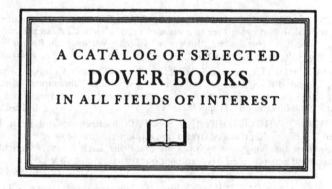

A CATALOG OF SELECTED
DOVER BOOKS
IN ALL FIELDS OF INTEREST

A CATALOG OF SELECTED DOVER
BOOKS IN ALL FIELDS OF INTEREST

100 BEST-LOVED POEMS, Edited by Philip Smith. "The Passionate Shepherd to His Love," "Shall I compare thee to a summer's day?" "Death, be not proud," "The Raven," "The Road Not Taken," plus works by Blake, Wordsworth, Byron, Shelley, Keats, many others. 96pp. 5⅟₁₆ x 8¼. 0-486-28553-7

100 SMALL HOUSES OF THE THIRTIES, Brown-Blodgett Company. Exterior photographs and floor plans for 100 charming structures. Illustrations of models accompanied by descriptions of interiors, color schemes, closet space, and other amenities. 200 illustrations. 112pp. 8⅜ x 11. 0-486-44131-8

1000 TURN-OF-THE-CENTURY HOUSES: With Illustrations and Floor Plans, Herbert C. Chivers. Reproduced from a rare edition, this showcase of homes ranges from cottages and bungalows to sprawling mansions. Each house is meticulously illustrated and accompanied by complete floor plans. 256pp. 9⅜ x 12¼.
0-486-45596-3

101 GREAT AMERICAN POEMS, Edited by The American Poetry & Literacy Project. Rich treasury of verse from the 19th and 20th centuries includes works by Edgar Allan Poe, Robert Frost, Walt Whitman, Langston Hughes, Emily Dickinson, T. S. Eliot, other notables. 96pp. 5⅟₁₆ x 8¼. 0-486-40158-8

101 GREAT SAMURAI PRINTS, Utagawa Kuniyoshi. Kuniyoshi was a master of the warrior woodblock print — and these 18th-century illustrations represent the pinnacle of his craft. Full-color portraits of renowned Japanese samurais pulse with movement, passion, and remarkably fine detail. 112pp. 8⅜ x 11. 0-486-46523-3

ABC OF BALLET, Janet Grosser. Clearly worded, abundantly illustrated little guide defines basic ballet-related terms: arabesque, battement, pas de chat, relevé, sissonne, many others. Pronunciation guide included. Excellent primer. 48pp. 4⅟₁₆ x 5¾.
0-486-40871-X

ACCESSORIES OF DRESS: An Illustrated Encyclopedia, Katherine Lester and Bess Viola Oerke. Illustrations of hats, veils, wigs, cravats, shawls, shoes, gloves, and other accessories enhance an engaging commentary that reveals the humor and charm of the many-sided story of accessorized apparel. 644 figures and 59 plates. 608pp. 6 ⅛ x 9¼.
0-486-43378-1

ADVENTURES OF HUCKLEBERRY FINN, Mark Twain. Join Huck and Jim as their boyhood adventures along the Mississippi River lead them into a world of excitement, danger, and self-discovery. Humorous narrative, lyrical descriptions of the Mississippi valley, and memorable characters. 224pp. 5⅟₁₆ x 8¼. 0-486-28061-6

ALICE STARMORE'S BOOK OF FAIR ISLE KNITTING, Alice Starmore. A noted designer from the region of Scotland's Fair Isle explores the history and techniques of this distinctive, stranded-color knitting style and provides copious illustrated instructions for 14 original knitwear designs. 208pp. 8⅜ x 10⅞. 0-486-47218-3

CATALOG OF DOVER BOOKS

ALICE'S ADVENTURES IN WONDERLAND, Lewis Carroll. Beloved classic about a little girl lost in a topsy-turvy land and her encounters with the White Rabbit, March Hare, Mad Hatter, Cheshire Cat, and other delightfully improbable characters. 42 illustrations by Sir John Tenniel. 96pp. 5⅜6 x 8¼. 0-486-27543-4

AMERICA'S LIGHTHOUSES: An Illustrated History, Francis Ross Holland. Profusely illustrated fact-filled survey of American lighthouses since 1716. Over 200 stations — East, Gulf, and West coasts, Great Lakes, Hawaii, Alaska, Puerto Rico, the Virgin Islands, and the Mississippi and St. Lawrence Rivers. 240pp. 8 x 10¾. 0-486-25576-X

AN ENCYCLOPEDIA OF THE VIOLIN, Alberto Bachmann. Translated by Frederick H. Martens. Introduction by Eugene Ysaye. First published in 1925, this renowned reference remains unsurpassed as a source of essential information, from construction and evolution to repertoire and technique. Includes a glossary and 73 illustrations. 496pp. 6½ x 9¼. 0-486-46618-3

ANIMALS: 1,419 Copyright-Free Illustrations of Mammals, Birds, Fish, Insects, etc., Selected by Jim Harter. Selected for its visual impact and ease of use, this outstanding collection of wood engravings presents over 1,000 species of animals in extremely lifelike poses. Includes mammals, birds, reptiles, amphibians, fish, insects, and other invertebrates. 284pp. 9 x 12. 0-486-23766-4

THE ANNALS, Tacitus. Translated by Alfred John Church and William Jackson Brodribb. This vital chronicle of Imperial Rome, written by the era's great historian, spans A.D. 14-68 and paints incisive psychological portraits of major figures, from Tiberius to Nero. 416pp. 5⅜6 x 8¼. 0-486-45236-0

ANTIGONE, Sophocles. Filled with passionate speeches and sensitive probing of moral and philosophical issues, this powerful and often-performed Greek drama reveals the grim fate that befalls the children of Oedipus. Footnotes. 64pp. 5⅜6 x 8 ¼. 0-486-27804-2

ART DECO DECORATIVE PATTERNS IN FULL COLOR, Christian Stoll. Reprinted from a rare 1910 portfolio, 160 sensuous and exotic images depict a breathtaking array of florals, geometrics, and abstracts — all elegant in their stark simplicity. 64pp. 8⅜ x 11. 0-486-44862-2

THE ARTHUR RACKHAM TREASURY: 86 Full-Color Illustrations, Arthur Rackham. Selected and Edited by Jeff A. Menges. A stunning treasury of 86 full-page plates span the famed English artist's career, from *Rip Van Winkle* (1905) to masterworks such as *Undine, A Midsummer Night's Dream*, and *Wind in the Willows* (1939). 96pp. 8⅜ x 11. 0-486-44685-9

THE AUTHENTIC GILBERT & SULLIVAN SONGBOOK, W. S. Gilbert and A. S. Sullivan. The most comprehensive collection available, this songbook includes selections from every one of Gilbert and Sullivan's light operas. Ninety-two numbers are presented uncut and unedited, and in their original keys. 410pp. 9 x 12. 0-486-23482-7

THE AWAKENING, Kate Chopin. First published in 1899, this controversial novel of a New Orleans wife's search for love outside a stifling marriage shocked readers. Today, it remains a first-rate narrative with superb characterization. New introductory Note. 128pp. 5⅜6 x 8¼. 0-486-27786-0

BASIC DRAWING, Louis Priscilla. Beginning with perspective, this commonsense manual progresses to the figure in movement, light and shade, anatomy, drapery, composition, trees and landscape, and outdoor sketching. Black-and-white illustrations throughout. 128pp. 8⅜ x 11. 0-486-45815-6

Browse over 9,000 books at www.doverpublications.com

THE BATTLES THAT CHANGED HISTORY, Fletcher Pratt. Historian profiles 16 crucial conflicts, ancient to modern, that changed the course of Western civilization. Gripping accounts of battles led by Alexander the Great, Joan of Arc, Ulysses S. Grant, other commanders. 27 maps. 352pp. 5⅜ x 8½.   0-486-41129-X

BEETHOVEN'S LETTERS, Ludwig van Beethoven. Edited by Dr. A. C. Kalischer. Features 457 letters to fellow musicians, friends, greats, patrons, and literary men. Reveals musical thoughts, quirks of personality, insights, and daily events. Includes 15 plates. 410pp. 5⅜ x 8½.   0-486-22769-3

BERNICE BOBS HER HAIR AND OTHER STORIES, F. Scott Fitzgerald. This brilliant anthology includes 6 of Fitzgerald's most popular stories: "The Diamond as Big as the Ritz," the title tale, "The Offshore Pirate," "The Ice Palace," "The Jelly Bean," and "May Day." 176pp. 5⅜ x 8½.   0-486-47049-0

BESLER'S BOOK OF FLOWERS AND PLANTS: 73 Full-Color Plates from Hortus Eystettensis, 1613, Basilius Besler. Here is a selection of magnificent plates from the *Hortus Eystettensis*, which vividly illustrated and identified the plants, flowers, and trees that thrived in the legendary German garden at Eichstätt. 80pp. 8⅜ x 11.
0-486-46005-3

THE BOOK OF KELLS, Edited by Blanche Cirker. Painstakingly reproduced from a rare facsimile edition, this volume contains full-page decorations, portraits, illustrations, plus a sampling of textual leaves with exquisite calligraphy and ornamentation. 32 full-color illustrations. 32pp. 9⅜ x 12¼.   0-486-24345-1

THE BOOK OF THE CROSSBOW: With an Additional Section on Catapults and Other Siege Engines, Ralph Payne-Gallwey. Fascinating study traces history and use of crossbow as military and sporting weapon, from Middle Ages to modern times. Also covers related weapons: balistas, catapults, Turkish bows, more. Over 240 illustrations. 400pp. 7¼ x 10⅛.   0-486-28720-3

THE BUNGALOW BOOK: Floor Plans and Photos of 112 Houses, 1910, Henry L. Wilson. Here are 112 of the most popular and economic blueprints of the early 20th century — plus an illustration or photograph of each completed house. A wonderful time capsule that still offers a wealth of valuable insights. 160pp. 8⅜ x 11.
0-486-45104-6

THE CALL OF THE WILD, Jack London. A classic novel of adventure, drawn from London's own experiences as a Klondike adventurer, relating the story of a heroic dog caught in the brutal life of the Alaska Gold Rush. Note. 64pp. 5³⁄₁₆ x 8¼.
0-486-26472-6

CANDIDE, Voltaire. Edited by Francois-Marie Arouet. One of the world's great satires since its first publication in 1759. Witty, caustic skewering of romance, science, philosophy, religion, government — nearly all human ideals and institutions. 112pp. 5³⁄₁₆ x 8¼.   0-486-26689-3

CELEBRATED IN THEIR TIME: Photographic Portraits from the George Grantham Bain Collection, Edited by Amy Pastan. With an Introduction by Michael Carlebach. Remarkable portrait gallery features 112 rare images of Albert Einstein, Charlie Chaplin, the Wright Brothers, Henry Ford, and other luminaries from the worlds of politics, art, entertainment, and industry. 128pp. 8⅜ x 11.   0-486-46754-6

CHARIOTS FOR APOLLO: The NASA History of Manned Lunar Spacecraft to 1969, Courtney G. Brooks, James M. Grimwood, and Loyd S. Swenson, Jr. This illustrated history by a trio of experts is the definitive reference on the Apollo spacecraft and lunar modules. It traces the vehicles' design, development, and operation in space. More than 100 photographs and illustrations. 576pp. 6¾ x 9¼. 0-486-46756-2

A CHRISTMAS CAROL, Charles Dickens. This engrossing tale relates Ebenezer Scrooge's ghostly journeys through Christmases past, present, and future and his ultimate transformation from a harsh and grasping old miser to a charitable and compassionate human being. 80pp. 5⅜₆ x 8¼. 0-486-26865-9

COMMON SENSE, Thomas Paine. First published in January of 1776, this highly influential landmark document clearly and persuasively argued for American separation from Great Britain and paved the way for the Declaration of Independence. 64pp. 5⅜₆ x 8¼. 0-486-29602-4

THE COMPLETE SHORT STORIES OF OSCAR WILDE, Oscar Wilde. Complete texts of "The Happy Prince and Other Tales," "A House of Pomegranates," "Lord Arthur Savile's Crime and Other Stories," "Poems in Prose," and "The Portrait of Mr. W. H." 208pp. 5⅜₆ x 8¼. 0-486-45216-6

COMPLETE SONNETS, William Shakespeare. Over 150 exquisite poems deal with love, friendship, the tyranny of time, beauty's evanescence, death, and other themes in language of remarkable power, precision, and beauty. Glossary of archaic terms. 80pp. 5⅜₆ x 8¼. 0-486-26686-9

THE COUNT OF MONTE CRISTO: Abridged Edition, Alexandre Dumas. Falsely accused of treason, Edmond Dantès is imprisoned in the bleak Chateau d'If. After a hair-raising escape, he launches an elaborate plot to extract a bitter revenge against those who betrayed him. 448pp. 5⅜₆ x 8¼. 0-486-45643-9

CRAFTSMAN BUNGALOWS: Designs from the Pacific Northwest, Yoho & Merritt. This reprint of a rare catalog, showcasing the charming simplicity and cozy style of Craftsman bungalows, is filled with photos of completed homes, plus floor plans and estimated costs. An indispensable resource for architects, historians, and illustrators. 112pp. 10 x 7. 0-486-46875-5

CRAFTSMAN BUNGALOWS: 59 Homes from "The Craftsman," Edited by Gustav Stickley. Best and most attractive designs from Arts and Crafts Movement publication — 1903–1916 — includes sketches, photographs of homes, floor plans, descriptive text. 128pp. 8¼ x 11. 0-486-25829-7

CRIME AND PUNISHMENT, Fyodor Dostoyevsky. Translated by Constance Garnett. Supreme masterpiece tells the story of Raskolnikov, a student tormented by his own thoughts after he murders an old woman. Overwhelmed by guilt and terror, he confesses and goes to prison. 480pp. 5⅜₆ x 8¼. 0-486-41587-2

THE DECLARATION OF INDEPENDENCE AND OTHER GREAT DOCUMENTS OF AMERICAN HISTORY: 1775-1865, Edited by John Grafton. Thirteen compelling and influential documents: Henry's "Give Me Liberty or Give Me Death," Declaration of Independence, The Constitution, Washington's First Inaugural Address, The Monroe Doctrine, The Emancipation Proclamation, Gettysburg Address, more. 64pp. 5⅜₆ x 8¼. 0-486-41124-9

THE DESERT AND THE SOWN: Travels in Palestine and Syria, Gertrude Bell. "The female Lawrence of Arabia," Gertrude Bell wrote captivating, perceptive accounts of her travels in the Middle East. This intriguing narrative, accompanied by 160 photos, traces her 1905 sojourn in Lebanon, Syria, and Palestine. 368pp. 5⅜ x 8½. 0-486-46876-3

A DOLL'S HOUSE, Henrik Ibsen. Ibsen's best-known play displays his genius for realistic prose drama. An expression of women's rights, the play climaxes when the central character, Nora, rejects a smothering marriage and life in "a doll's house." 80pp. 5⅜₆ x 8¼. 0-486-27062-9

DOOMED SHIPS: Great Ocean Liner Disasters, William H. Miller, Jr. Nearly 200 photographs, many from private collections, highlight tales of some of the vessels whose pleasure cruises ended in catastrophe: the *Morro Castle, Normandie, Andrea Doria, Europa,* and many others. 128pp. 8⅞ x 11¼. 0-486-45366-9

THE DORÉ BIBLE ILLUSTRATIONS, Gustave Doré. Detailed plates from the Bible: the Creation scenes, Adam and Eve, horrifying visions of the Flood, the battle sequences with their monumental crowds, depictions of the life of Jesus, 241 plates in all. 241pp. 9 x 12. 0-486-23004-X

DRAWING DRAPERY FROM HEAD TO TOE, Cliff Young. Expert guidance on how to draw shirts, pants, skirts, gloves, hats, and coats on the human figure, including folds in relation to the body, pull and crush, action folds, creases, more. Over 200 drawings. 48pp. 8¼ x 11. 0-486-45591-2

DUBLINERS, James Joyce. A fine and accessible introduction to the work of one of the 20th century's most influential writers, this collection features 15 tales, including a masterpiece of the short-story genre, "The Dead." 160pp. 5³⁄₁₆ x 8¼.
0-486-26870-5

EASY-TO-MAKE POP-UPS, Joan Irvine. Illustrated by Barbara Reid. Dozens of wonderful ideas for three-dimensional paper fun — from holiday greeting cards with moving parts to a pop-up menagerie. Easy-to-follow, illustrated instructions for more than 30 projects. 299 black-and-white illustrations. 96pp. 8⅜ x 11.
0-486-44622-0

EASY-TO-MAKE STORYBOOK DOLLS: A "Novel" Approach to Cloth Dollmaking, Sherralyn St. Clair. Favorite fictional characters come alive in this unique beginner's dollmaking guide. Includes patterns for Pollyanna, Dorothy from *The Wonderful Wizard of Oz*, Mary of *The Secret Garden*, plus easy-to-follow instructions, 263 black-and-white illustrations, and an 8-page color insert. 112pp. 8¼ x 11. 0-486-47360-0

EINSTEIN'S ESSAYS IN SCIENCE, Albert Einstein. Speeches and essays in accessible, everyday language profile influential physicists such as Niels Bohr and Isaac Newton. They also explore areas of physics to which the author made major contributions. 128pp. 5 x 8. 0-486-47011-3

EL DORADO: Further Adventures of the Scarlet Pimpernel, Baroness Orczy. A popular sequel to *The Scarlet Pimpernel*, this suspenseful story recounts the Pimpernel's attempts to rescue the Dauphin from imprisonment during the French Revolution. An irresistible blend of intrigue, period detail, and vibrant characterizations. 352pp. 5³⁄₁₆ x 8¼. 0-486-44026-5

ELEGANT SMALL HOMES OF THE TWENTIES: 99 Designs from a Competition, Chicago Tribune. Nearly 100 designs for five- and six-room houses feature New England and Southern colonials, Normandy cottages, stately Italianate dwellings, and other fascinating snapshots of American domestic architecture of the 1920s. 112pp. 9 x 12. 0-486-46910-7

THE ELEMENTS OF STYLE: The Original Edition, William Strunk, Jr. This is the book that generations of writers have relied upon for timeless advice on grammar, diction, syntax, and other essentials. In concise terms, it identifies the principal requirements of proper style and common errors. 64pp. 5⅜ x 8½. 0-486-44798-7

THE ELUSIVE PIMPERNEL, Baroness Orczy. Robespierre's revolutionaries find their wicked schemes thwarted by the heroic Pimpernel — Sir Percival Blakeney. In this thrilling sequel, Chauvelin devises a plot to eliminate the Pimpernel and his wife. 272pp. 5³⁄₁₆ x 8¼. 0-486-45464-9

AN ENCYCLOPEDIA OF BATTLES: Accounts of Over 1,560 Battles from 1479 B.C. to the Present, David Eggenberger. Essential details of every major battle in recorded history from the first battle of Megiddo in 1479 B.C. to Grenada in 1984. List of battle maps. 99 illustrations. 544pp. 6½ x 9¼. 0-486-24913-1

ENCYCLOPEDIA OF EMBROIDERY STITCHES, INCLUDING CREWEL, Marion Nichols. Precise explanations and instructions, clearly illustrated, on how to work chain, back, cross, knotted, woven stitches, and many more — 178 in all, including Cable Outline, Whipped Satin, and Eyelet Buttonhole. Over 1400 illustrations. 219pp. 8⅜ x 11¼. 0-486-22929-7

ENTER JEEVES: 15 Early Stories, P. G. Wodehouse. Splendid collection contains first 8 stories featuring Bertie Wooster, the deliciously dim aristocrat and Jeeves, his brainy, imperturbable manservant. Also, the complete Reggie Pepper (Bertie's prototype) series. 288pp. 5⅜ x 8½. 0-486-29717-9

ERIC SLOANE'S AMERICA: Paintings in Oil, Michael Wigley. With a Foreword by Mimi Sloane. Eric Sloane's evocative oils of America's landscape and material culture shimmer with immense historical and nostalgic appeal. This original hardcover collection gathers nearly a hundred of his finest paintings, with subjects ranging from New England to the American Southwest. 128pp. 10⅝ x 9.
0-486-46525-X

ETHAN FROME, Edith Wharton. Classic story of wasted lives, set against a bleak New England background. Superbly delineated characters in a hauntingly grim tale of thwarted love. Considered by many to be Wharton's masterpiece. 96pp. 5 9/16 x 8 ¼.
0-486-26690-7

THE EVERLASTING MAN, G. K. Chesterton. Chesterton's view of Christianity — as a blend of philosophy and mythology, satisfying intellect and spirit — applies to his brilliant book, which appeals to readers' heads as well as their hearts. 288pp. 5⅜ x 8½.
0-486-46036-3

THE FIELD AND FOREST HANDY BOOK, Daniel Beard. Written by a co-founder of the Boy Scouts, this appealing guide offers illustrated instructions for building kites, birdhouses, boats, igloos, and other fun projects, plus numerous helpful tips for campers. 448pp. 5 9/16 x 8¼. 0-486-46191-2

FINDING YOUR WAY WITHOUT MAP OR COMPASS, Harold Gatty. Useful, instructive manual shows would-be explorers, hikers, bikers, scouts, sailors, and survivalists how to find their way outdoors by observing animals, weather patterns, shifting sands, and other elements of nature. 288pp. 5⅜ x 8½. 0-486-40613-X

FIRST FRENCH READER: A Beginner's Dual-Language Book, Edited and Translated by Stanley Appelbaum. This anthology introduces 50 legendary writers — Voltaire, Balzac, Baudelaire, Proust, more — through passages from *The Red and the Black, Les Misérables, Madame Bovary*, and other classics. Original French text plus English translation on facing pages. 240pp. 5⅜ x 8½. 0-486-46178-5

FIRST GERMAN READER: A Beginner's Dual-Language Book, Edited by Harry Steinhauer. Specially chosen for their power to evoke German life and culture, these short, simple readings include poems, stories, essays, and anecdotes by Goethe, Hesse, Heine, Schiller, and others. 224pp. 5⅜ x 8½. 0-486-46179-3

FIRST SPANISH READER: A Beginner's Dual-Language Book, Angel Flores. Delightful stories, other material based on works of Don Juan Manuel, Luis Taboada, Ricardo Palma, other noted writers. Complete faithful English translations on facing pages. Exercises. 176pp. 5⅜ x 8½. 0-486-25810-6

FIVE ACRES AND INDEPENDENCE, Maurice G. Kains. Great back-to-the-land classic explains basics of self-sufficient farming. The one book to get. 95 illustrations. 397pp. 5⅜ x 8½. 0-486-20974-1

FLAGG'S SMALL HOUSES: Their Economic Design and Construction, 1922, Ernest Flagg. Although most famous for his skyscrapers, Flagg was also a proponent of the well-designed single-family dwelling. His classic treatise features innovations that save space, materials, and cost. 526 illustrations. 160pp. 9⅜ x 12¼.
0-486-45197-6

FLATLAND: A Romance of Many Dimensions, Edwin A. Abbott. Classic of science (and mathematical) fiction — charmingly illustrated by the author — describes the adventures of A. Square, a resident of Flatland, in Spaceland (three dimensions), Lineland (one dimension), and Pointland (no dimensions). 96pp. 5³⁄₁₆ x 8¼.
0-486-27263-X

FRANKENSTEIN, Mary Shelley. The story of Victor Frankenstein's monstrous creation and the havoc it caused has enthralled generations of readers and inspired countless writers of horror and suspense. With the author's own 1831 introduction. 176pp. 5³⁄₁₆ x 8¼. 0-486-28211-2

THE GARGOYLE BOOK: 572 Examples from Gothic Architecture, Lester Burbank Bridaham. Dispelling the conventional wisdom that French Gothic architectural flourishes were born of despair or gloom, Bridaham reveals the whimsical nature of these creations and the ingenious artisans who made them. 572 illustrations. 224pp. 8⅜ x 11. 0-486-44754-5

THE GIFT OF THE MAGI AND OTHER SHORT STORIES, O. Henry. Sixteen captivating stories by one of America's most popular storytellers. Included are such classics as "The Gift of the Magi," "The Last Leaf," and "The Ransom of Red Chief." Publisher's Note. 96pp. 5³⁄₁₆ x 8¼. 0-486-27061-0

THE GOETHE TREASURY: Selected Prose and Poetry, Johann Wolfgang von Goethe. Edited, Selected, and with an Introduction by Thomas Mann. In addition to his lyric poetry, Goethe wrote travel sketches, autobiographical studies, essays, letters, and proverbs in rhyme and prose. This collection presents outstanding examples from each genre. 368pp. 5⅜ x 8½. 0-486-44780-4

GREAT EXPECTATIONS, Charles Dickens. Orphaned Pip is apprenticed to the dirty work of the forge but dreams of becoming a gentleman — and one day finds himself in possession of "great expectations." Dickens' finest novel. 400pp. 5³⁄₁₆ x 8¼.
0-486-41586-4

GREAT WRITERS ON THE ART OF FICTION: From Mark Twain to Joyce Carol Oates, Edited by James Daley. An indispensable source of advice and inspiration, this anthology features essays by Henry James, Kate Chopin, Willa Cather, Sinclair Lewis, Jack London, Raymond Chandler, Raymond Carver, Eudora Welty, and Kurt Vonnegut, Jr. 192pp. 5⅜ x 8½. 0-486-45128-3

HAMLET, William Shakespeare. The quintessential Shakespearean tragedy, whose highly charged confrontations and anguished soliloquies probe depths of human feeling rarely sounded in any art. Reprinted from an authoritative British edition complete with illuminating footnotes. 128pp. 5³⁄₁₆ x 8¼. 0-486-27278-8

THE HAUNTED HOUSE, Charles Dickens. A Yuletide gathering in an eerie country retreat provides the backdrop for Dickens and his friends — including Elizabeth Gaskell and Wilkie Collins — who take turns spinning supernatural yarns. 144pp. 5⅜ x 8½. 0-486-46309-5

HEART OF DARKNESS, Joseph Conrad. Dark allegory of a journey up the Congo River and the narrator's encounter with the mysterious Mr. Kurtz. Masterly blend of adventure, character study, psychological penetration. For many, Conrad's finest, most enigmatic story. 80pp. 5³⁄₁₆ x 8¼. 0-486-26464-5

HENSON AT THE NORTH POLE, Matthew A. Henson. This thrilling memoir by the heroic African-American who was Peary's companion through two decades of Arctic exploration recounts a tale of danger, courage, and determination. "Fascinating and exciting." — *Commonweal.* 128pp. 5⅜ x 8½. 0-486-45472-X

HISTORIC COSTUMES AND HOW TO MAKE THEM, Mary Fernald and E. Shenton. Practical, informative guidebook shows how to create everything from short tunics worn by Saxon men in the fifth century to a lady's bustle dress of the late 1800s. 81 illustrations. 176pp. 5⅜ x 8½. 0-486-44906-8

THE HOUND OF THE BASKERVILLES, Arthur Conan Doyle. A deadly curse in the form of a legendary ferocious beast continues to claim its victims from the Baskerville family until Holmes and Watson intervene. Often called the best detective story ever written. 128pp. 5³⁄₁₆ x 8¼. 0-486-28214-7

THE HOUSE BEHIND THE CEDARS, Charles W. Chesnutt. Originally published in 1900, this groundbreaking novel by a distinguished African-American author recounts the drama of a brother and sister who "pass for white" during the dangerous days of Reconstruction. 208pp. 5⅜ x 8½. 0-486-46144-0

THE HUMAN FIGURE IN MOTION, Eadweard Muybridge. The 4,789 photographs in this definitive selection show the human figure — models almost all undraped — engaged in over 160 different types of action: running, climbing stairs, etc. 390pp. 7⅞ x 10⅝. 0-486-20204-6

THE IMPORTANCE OF BEING EARNEST, Oscar Wilde. Wilde's witty and buoyant comedy of manners, filled with some of literature's most famous epigrams, reprinted from an authoritative British edition. Considered Wilde's most perfect work. 64pp. 5³⁄₁₆ x 8¼. 0-486-26478-5

THE INFERNO, Dante Alighieri. Translated and with notes by Henry Wadsworth Longfellow. The first stop on Dante's famous journey from Hell to Purgatory to Paradise, this 14th-century allegorical poem blends vivid and shocking imagery with graceful lyricism. Translated by the beloved 19th-century poet, Henry Wadsworth Longfellow. 256pp. 5³⁄₁₆ x 8¼. 0-486-44288-8

JANE EYRE, Charlotte Brontë. Written in 1847, *Jane Eyre* tells the tale of an orphan girl's progress from the custody of cruel relatives to an oppressive boarding school and its culmination in a troubled career as a governess. 448pp. 5³⁄₁₆ x 8¼.
0-486-42449-9

JAPANESE WOODBLOCK FLOWER PRINTS, Tanigami Kônan. Extraordinary collection of Japanese woodblock prints by a well-known artist features 120 plates in brilliant color. Realistic images from a rare edition include daffodils, tulips, and other familiar and unusual flowers. 128pp. 11 x 8¼. 0-486-46442-3

JEWELRY MAKING AND DESIGN, Augustus F. Rose and Antonio Cirino. Professional secrets of jewelry making are revealed in a thorough, practical guide. Over 200 illustrations. 306pp. 5⅜ x 8½. 0-486-21750-7

JULIUS CAESAR, William Shakespeare. Great tragedy based on Plutarch's account of the lives of Brutus, Julius Caesar and Mark Antony. Evil plotting, ringing oratory, high tragedy with Shakespeare's incomparable insight, dramatic power. Explanatory footnotes. 96pp. 5³⁄₁₆ x 8¼. 0-486-26876-4

THE JUNGLE, Upton Sinclair. 1906 bestseller shockingly reveals intolerable labor practices and working conditions in the Chicago stockyards as it tells the grim story of a Slavic family that emigrates to America full of optimism but soon faces despair. 320pp. 5³⁄₁₆ x 8¼. 0-486-41923-1

THE KINGDOM OF GOD IS WITHIN YOU, Leo Tolstoy. The soul-searching book that inspired Gandhi to embrace the concept of passive resistance, Tolstoy's 1894 polemic clearly outlines a radical, well-reasoned revision of traditional Christian thinking. 352pp. 5³⁄₁₆ x 8¼. 0-486-45138-0

THE LADY OR THE TIGER?: and Other Logic Puzzles, Raymond M. Smullyan. Created by a renowned puzzle master, these whimsically themed challenges involve paradoxes about probability, time, and change; metapuzzles; and self-referentiality. Nineteen chapters advance in difficulty from relatively simple to highly complex. 1982 edition. 240pp. 5⅜ x 8½. 0-486-47027-X

LEAVES OF GRASS: The Original 1855 Edition, Walt Whitman. Whitman's immortal collection includes some of the greatest poems of modern times, including his masterpiece, "Song of Myself." Shattering standard conventions, it stands as an unabashed celebration of body and nature. 128pp. 5³⁄₁₆ x 8¼. 0-486-45676-5

LES MISÉRABLES, Victor Hugo. Translated by Charles E. Wilbour. Abridged by James K. Robinson. A convict's heroic struggle for justice and redemption plays out against a fiery backdrop of the Napoleonic wars. This edition features the excellent original translation and a sensitive abridgment. 304pp. 6⅛ x 9¼. 0-486-45789-3

LILITH: A Romance, George MacDonald. In this novel by the father of fantasy literature, a man travels through time to meet Adam and Eve and to explore humanity's fall from grace and ultimate redemption. 240pp. 5⅜ x 8½. 0-486-46818-6

THE LOST LANGUAGE OF SYMBOLISM, Harold Bayley. This remarkable book reveals the hidden meaning behind familiar images and words, from the origins of Santa Claus to the fleur-de-lys, drawing from mythology, folklore, religious texts, and fairy tales. 1,418 illustrations. 784pp. 5⅜ x 8½. 0-486-44787-1

MACBETH, William Shakespeare. A Scottish nobleman murders the king in order to succeed to the throne. Tortured by his conscience and fearful of discovery, he becomes tangled in a web of treachery and deceit that ultimately spells his doom. 96pp. 5³⁄₁₆ x 8¼. 0-486-27802-6

MAKING AUTHENTIC CRAFTSMAN FURNITURE: Instructions and Plans for 62 Projects, Gustav Stickley. Make authentic reproductions of handsome, functional, durable furniture: tables, chairs, wall cabinets, desks, a hall tree, and more. Construction plans with drawings, schematics, dimensions, and lumber specs reprinted from 1900s The Craftsman magazine. 128pp. 8⅛ x 11. 0-486-25000-8

MATHEMATICS FOR THE NONMATHEMATICIAN, Morris Kline. Erudite and entertaining overview follows development of mathematics from ancient Greeks to present. Topics include logic and mathematics, the fundamental concept, differential calculus, probability theory, much more. Exercises and problems. 641pp. 5⅜ x 8½. 0-486-24823-2

MEMOIRS OF AN ARABIAN PRINCESS FROM ZANZIBAR, Emily Ruete. This 19th-century autobiography offers a rare inside look at the society surrounding a sultan's palace. A real-life princess in exile recalls her vanished world of harems, slave trading, and court intrigues. 288pp. 5⅜ x 8½. 0-486-47121-7

THE METAMORPHOSIS AND OTHER STORIES, Franz Kafka. Excellent new English translations of title story (considered by many critics Kafka's most perfect work), plus "The Judgment," "In the Penal Colony," "A Country Doctor," and "A Report to an Academy." Note. 96pp. 5¾6 x 8¼. 0-486-29030-1

MICROSCOPIC ART FORMS FROM THE PLANT WORLD, R. Anheisser. From undulating curves to complex geometrics, a world of fascinating images abound in this classic, illustrated survey of microscopic plants. Features 400 detailed illustrations of nature's minute but magnificent handiwork. The accompanying CD-ROM includes all of the images in the book. 128pp. 9 x 9. 0-486-46013-4

A MIDSUMMER NIGHT'S DREAM, William Shakespeare. Among the most popular of Shakespeare's comedies, this enchanting play humorously celebrates the vagaries of love as it focuses upon the intertwined romances of several pairs of lovers. Explanatory footnotes. 80pp. 5¾6 x 8¼. 0-486-27067-X

THE MONEY CHANGERS, Upton Sinclair. Originally published in 1908, this cautionary novel from the author of *The Jungle* explores corruption within the American system as a group of power brokers joins forces for personal gain, triggering a crash on Wall Street. 192pp. 5⅜ x 8½. 0-486-46917-4

THE MOST POPULAR HOMES OF THE TWENTIES, William A. Radford. With a New Introduction by Daniel D. Reiff. Based on a rare 1925 catalog, this architectural showcase features floor plans, construction details, and photos of 26 homes, plus articles on entrances, porches, garages, and more. 250 illustrations, 21 color plates. 176pp. 8⅜ x 11. 0-486-47028-8

MY 66 YEARS IN THE BIG LEAGUES, Connie Mack. With a New Introduction by Rich Westcott. A Founding Father of modern baseball, Mack holds the record for most wins — and losses — by a major league manager. Enhanced by 70 photographs, his warmhearted autobiography is populated by many legends of the game. 288pp. 5⅜ x 8½. 0-486-47184-5

NARRATIVE OF THE LIFE OF FREDERICK DOUGLASS, Frederick Douglass. Douglass's graphic depictions of slavery, harrowing escape to freedom, and life as a newspaper editor, eloquent orator, and impassioned abolitionist. 96pp. 5¾6 x 8¼. 0-486-28499-9

THE NIGHTLESS CITY: Geisha and Courtesan Life in Old Tokyo, J. E. de Becker. This unsurpassed study from 100 years ago ventured into Tokyo's red-light district to survey geisha and courtesan life and offer meticulous descriptions of training, dress, social hierarchy, and erotic practices. 49 black-and-white illustrations; 2 maps. 496pp. 5⅜ x 8½. 0-486-45563-7

THE ODYSSEY, Homer. Excellent prose translation of ancient epic recounts adventures of the homeward-bound Odysseus. Fantastic cast of gods, giants, cannibals, sirens, other supernatural creatures — true classic of Western literature. 256pp. 5¾6 x 8¼. 0-486-40654-7

OEDIPUS REX, Sophocles. Landmark of Western drama concerns the catastrophe that ensues when King Oedipus discovers he has inadvertently killed his father and married his mother. Masterly construction, dramatic irony. Explanatory footnotes. 64pp. 5¾6 x 8¼. 0-486-26877-2

ONCE UPON A TIME: The Way America Was, Eric Sloane. Nostalgic text and drawings brim with gentle philosophies and descriptions of how we used to live — self-sufficiently — on the land, in homes, and among the things built by hand. 44 line illustrations. 64pp. 8⅜ x 11. 0-486-44411-2

ONE OF OURS, Willa Cather. The Pulitzer Prize–winning novel about a young Nebraskan looking for something to believe in. Alienated from his parents, rejected by his wife, he finds his destiny on the bloody battlefields of World War I. 352pp. 5⅜6 x 8¼. 0-486-45599-8

ORIGAMI YOU CAN USE: 27 Practical Projects, Rick Beech. Origami models can be more than decorative, and this unique volume shows how! The 27 practical projects include a CD case, frame, napkin ring, and dish. Easy instructions feature 400 two-color illustrations. 96pp. 8¼ x 11. 0-486-47057-1

OTHELLO, William Shakespeare. Towering tragedy tells the story of a Moorish general who earns the enmity of his ensign Iago when he passes him over for a promotion. Masterly portrait of an archvillain. Explanatory footnotes. 112pp. 5⅜6 x 8¼. 0-486-29097-2

PARADISE LOST, John Milton. Notes by John A. Himes. First published in 1667, *Paradise Lost* ranks among the greatest of English literature's epic poems. It's a sublime retelling of Adam and Eve's fall from grace and expulsion from Eden. Notes by John A. Himes. 480pp. 5⅜6 x 8¼. 0-486-44287-X

PASSING, Nella Larsen. Married to a successful physician and prominently ensconced in society, Irene Redfield leads a charmed existence — until a chance encounter with a childhood friend who has been "passing for white." 112pp. 5⅜ x 8½. 0-486-43713-2

PERSPECTIVE DRAWING FOR BEGINNERS, Len A. Doust. Doust carefully explains the roles of lines, boxes, and circles, and shows how visualizing shapes and forms can be used in accurate depictions of perspective. One of the most concise introductions available. 33 illustrations. 64pp. 5⅜ x 8½. 0-486-45149-6

PERSPECTIVE MADE EASY, Ernest R. Norling. Perspective is easy; yet, surprisingly few artists know the simple rules that make it so. Remedy that situation with this simple, step-by-step book, the first devoted entirely to the topic. 256 illustrations. 224pp. 5⅜ x 8½. 0-486-40473-0

THE PICTURE OF DORIAN GRAY, Oscar Wilde. Celebrated novel involves a handsome young Londoner who sinks into a life of depravity. His body retains perfect youth and vigor while his recent portrait reflects the ravages of his crime and sensuality. 176pp. 5⅜6 x 8¼. 0-486-27807-7

PRIDE AND PREJUDICE, Jane Austen. One of the most universally loved and admired English novels, an effervescent tale of rural romance transformed by Jane Austen's art into a witty, shrewdly observed satire of English country life. 272pp. 5⅜6 x 8¼. 0-486-28473-5

THE PRINCE, Niccolò Machiavelli. Classic, Renaissance-era guide to acquiring and maintaining political power. Today, nearly 500 years after it was written, this calculating prescription for autocratic rule continues to be much read and studied. 80pp. 5⅜6 x 8¼. 0-486-27274-5

QUICK SKETCHING, Carl Cheek. A perfect introduction to the technique of "quick sketching." Drawing upon an artist's immediate emotional responses, this is an extremely effective means of capturing the essential form and features of a subject. More than 100 black-and-white illustrations throughout. 48pp. 11 x 8¼. 0-486-46608-6

RANCH LIFE AND THE HUNTING TRAIL, Theodore Roosevelt. Illustrated by Frederic Remington. Beautifully illustrated by Remington, Roosevelt's celebration of the Old West recounts his adventures in the Dakota Badlands of the 1880s, from roundups to Indian encounters to hunting bighorn sheep. 208pp. 6¼ x 9¼. 0-486-47340-6

THE RED BADGE OF COURAGE, Stephen Crane. Amid the nightmarish chaos of a Civil War battle, a young soldier discovers courage, humility, and, perhaps, wisdom. Uncanny re-creation of actual combat. Enduring landmark of American fiction. 112pp. 5³⁄₁₆ x 8¼. 0-486-26465-3

RELATIVITY SIMPLY EXPLAINED, Martin Gardner. One of the subject's clearest, most entertaining introductions offers lucid explanations of special and general theories of relativity, gravity, and spacetime, models of the universe, and more. 100 illustrations. 224pp. 5⅜ x 8½. 0-486-29315-7

REMBRANDT DRAWINGS: 116 Masterpieces in Original Color, Rembrandt van Rijn. This deluxe hardcover edition features drawings from throughout the Dutch master's prolific career. Informative captions accompany these beautifully reproduced landscapes, biblical vignettes, figure studies, animal sketches, and portraits. 128pp. 8⅜ x 11. 0-486-46149-1

THE ROAD NOT TAKEN AND OTHER POEMS, Robert Frost. A treasury of Frost's most expressive verse. In addition to the title poem: "An Old Man's Winter Night," "In the Home Stretch," "Meeting and Passing," "Putting in the Seed," many more. All complete and unabridged. 64pp. 5³⁄₁₆ x 8¼. 0-486-27550-7

ROMEO AND JULIET, William Shakespeare. Tragic tale of star-crossed lovers, feuding families and timeless passion contains some of Shakespeare's most beautiful and lyrical love poetry. Complete, unabridged text with explanatory footnotes. 96pp. 5³⁄₁₆ x 8¼. 0-486-27557-4

SANDITON AND THE WATSONS: Austen's Unfinished Novels, Jane Austen. Two tantalizing incomplete stories revisit Austen's customary milieu of courtship and venture into new territory, amid guests at a seaside resort. Both are worth reading for pleasure and study. 112pp. 5⅜ x 8½. 0-486-45793-1

THE SCARLET LETTER, Nathaniel Hawthorne. With stark power and emotional depth, Hawthorne's masterpiece explores sin, guilt, and redemption in a story of adultery in the early days of the Massachusetts Colony. 192pp. 5³⁄₁₆ x 8¼.
0-486-28048-9

THE SEASONS OF AMERICA PAST, Eric Sloane. Seventy-five illustrations depict cider mills and presses, sleds, pumps, stump-pulling equipment, plows, and other elements of America's rural heritage. A section of old recipes and household hints adds additional color. 160pp. 8⅜ x 11. 0-486-44220-9

SELECTED CANTERBURY TALES, Geoffrey Chaucer. Delightful collection includes the General Prologue plus three of the most popular tales: "The Knight's Tale," "The Miller's Prologue and Tale," and "The Wife of Bath's Prologue and Tale." In modern English. 144pp. 5³⁄₁₆ x 8¼. 0-486-28241-4

SELECTED POEMS, Emily Dickinson. Over 100 best-known, best-loved poems by one of America's foremost poets, reprinted from authoritative early editions. No comparable edition at this price. Index of first lines. 64pp. 5³⁄₁₆ x 8¼. 0-486-26466-1

SIDDHARTHA, Hermann Hesse. Classic novel that has inspired generations of seekers. Blending Eastern mysticism and psychoanalysis, Hesse presents a strikingly original view of man and culture and the arduous process of self-discovery, reconciliation, harmony, and peace. 112pp. 5³⁄₁₆ x 8¼. 0-486-40653-9

SKETCHING OUTDOORS, Leonard Richmond. This guide offers beginners step-by-step demonstrations of how to depict clouds, trees, buildings, and other outdoor sights. Explanations of a variety of techniques include shading and constructional drawing. 48pp. 11 x 8¼. 0-486-46922-0

Browse over 9,000 books at www.doverpublications.com

SMALL HOUSES OF THE FORTIES: With Illustrations and Floor Plans, Harold E. Group. 56 floor plans and elevations of houses that originally cost less than $15,000 to build. Recommended by financial institutions of the era, they range from Colonials to Cape Cods. 144pp. 8⅜ x 11. 0-486-45598-X

SOME CHINESE GHOSTS, Lafcadio Hearn. Rooted in ancient Chinese legends, these richly atmospheric supernatural tales are recounted by an expert in Oriental lore. Their originality, power, and literary charm will captivate readers of all ages. 96pp. 5⅜ x 8½. 0-486-46306-0

SONGS FOR THE OPEN ROAD: Poems of Travel and Adventure, Edited by The American Poetry & Literacy Project. More than 80 poems by 50 American and British masters celebrate real and metaphorical journeys. Poems by Whitman, Byron, Millay, Sandburg, Langston Hughes, Emily Dickinson, Robert Frost, Shelley, Tennyson, Yeats, many others. Note. 80pp. 5³⁄₁₆ x 8¼. 0-486-40646-6

SPOON RIVER ANTHOLOGY, Edgar Lee Masters. An American poetry classic, in which former citizens of a mythical midwestern town speak touchingly from the grave of the thwarted hopes and dreams of their lives. 144pp. 5³⁄₁₆ x 8¼. 0-486-27275-3

STAR LORE: Myths, Legends, and Facts, William Tyler Olcott. Captivating retellings of the origins and histories of ancient star groups include Pegasus, Ursa Major, Pleiades, signs of the zodiac, and other constellations. "Classic." — *Sky & Telescope*. 58 illustrations. 544pp. 5⅜ x 8½. 0-486-43581-4

THE STRANGE CASE OF DR. JEKYLL AND MR. HYDE, Robert Louis Stevenson. This intriguing novel, both fantasy thriller and moral allegory, depicts the struggle of two opposing personalities — one essentially good, the other evil — for the soul of one man. 64pp. 5³⁄₁₆ x 8¼. 0-486-26688-5

SURVIVAL HANDBOOK: The Official U.S. Army Guide, Department of the Army. This special edition of the Army field manual is geared toward civilians. An essential companion for campers and all lovers of the outdoors, it constitutes the most authoritative wilderness guide. 288pp. 5³⁄₁₆ x 8¼. 0-486-46184-X

A TALE OF TWO CITIES, Charles Dickens. Against the backdrop of the French Revolution, Dickens unfolds his masterpiece of drama, adventure, and romance about a man falsely accused of treason. Excitement and derring-do in the shadow of the guillotine. 304pp. 5³⁄₁₆ x 8¼. 0-486-40651-2

TEN PLAYS, Anton Chekhov. *The Sea Gull, Uncle Vanya, The Three Sisters, The Cherry Orchard*, and *Ivanov*, plus 5 one-act comedies: *The Anniversary, An Unwilling Martyr, The Wedding, The Bear*, and *The Proposal*. 336pp. 5³⁄₁₆ x 8¼. 0-486-46560-8

THE FLYING INN, G. K. Chesterton. Hilarious romp in which pub owner Humphrey Hump and friend take to the road in a donkey cart filled with rum and cheese, inveighing against Prohibition and other "oppressive forms of modernity." 320pp. 5⅜ x 8½. 0-486-41910-X

THIRTY YEARS THAT SHOOK PHYSICS: The Story of Quantum Theory, George Gamow. Lucid, accessible introduction to the influential theory of energy and matter features careful explanations of Dirac's anti-particles, Bohr's model of the atom, and much more. Numerous drawings. 1966 edition. 240pp. 5⅜ x 8½. 0-486-24895-X

TREASURE ISLAND, Robert Louis Stevenson. Classic adventure story of a perilous sea journey, a mutiny led by the infamous Long John Silver, and a lethal scramble for buried treasure — seen through the eyes of cabin boy Jim Hawkins. 160pp. 5³⁄₁₆ x 8¼. 0-486-27559-0

THE TRIAL, Franz Kafka. Translated by David Wyllie. From its gripping first sentence onward, this novel exemplifies the term "Kafkaesque." Its darkly humorous narrative recounts a bank clerk's entrapment in a bureaucratic maze, based on an undisclosed charge. 176pp. 5³⁄₁₆ x 8¼.   0-486-47061-X

THE TURN OF THE SCREW, Henry James. Gripping ghost story by great novelist depicts the sinister transformation of 2 innocent children into flagrant liars and hypocrites. An elegantly told tale of unspoken horror and psychological terror. 96pp. 5³⁄₁₆ x 8¼.   0-486-26684-2

UP FROM SLAVERY, Booker T. Washington. Washington (1856-1915) rose to become the most influential spokesman for African-Americans of his day. In this eloquently written book, he describes events in a remarkable life that began in bondage and culminated in worldwide recognition. 160pp. 5³⁄₁₆ x 8¼.   0-486-28738-6

VICTORIAN HOUSE DESIGNS IN AUTHENTIC FULL COLOR: 75 Plates from the "Scientific American – Architects and Builders Edition," 1885-1894, Edited by Blanche Cirker. Exquisitely detailed, exceptionally handsome designs for an enormous variety of attractive city dwellings, spacious suburban and country homes, charming "cottages" and other structures — all accompanied by perspective views and floor plans. 80pp. 9¼ x 12¼.   0-486-29438-2

VILLETTE, Charlotte Brontë. Acclaimed by Virginia Woolf as "Brontë's finest novel," this moving psychological study features a remarkably modern heroine who abandons her native England for a new life as a schoolteacher in Belgium. 480pp. 5³⁄₁₆ x 8¼.   0-486-45557-2

THE VOYAGE OUT, Virginia Woolf. A moving depiction of the thrills and confusion of youth, Woolf's acclaimed first novel traces a shipboard journey to South America for a captivating exploration of a woman's growing self-awareness. 288pp. 5³⁄₁₆ x 8¼.   0-486-45005-8

WALDEN; OR, LIFE IN THE WOODS, Henry David Thoreau. Accounts of Thoreau's daily life on the shores of Walden Pond outside Concord, Massachusetts, are interwoven with musings on the virtues of self-reliance and individual freedom, on society, government, and other topics. 224pp. 5³⁄₁₆ x 8¼.   0-486-28495-6

WILD PILGRIMAGE: A Novel in Woodcuts, Lynd Ward. Through startling engravings shaded in black and red, Ward wordlessly tells the story of a man trapped in an industrial world, struggling between the grim reality around him and the fantasies his imagination creates. 112pp. 6⅛ x 9¼.   0-486-46583-7

WILLY POGÁNY REDISCOVERED, Willy Pogány. Selected and Edited by Jeff A. Menges. More than 100 color and black-and-white Art Nouveau–style illustrations from fairy tales and adventure stories include scenes from Wagner's "Ring" cycle, *The Rime of the Ancient Mariner, Gulliver's Travels,* and *Faust.* 144pp. 8⅜ x 11.
                                   0-486-47046-6

WOOLLY THOUGHTS: Unlock Your Creative Genius with Modular Knitting, Pat Ashforth and Steve Plummer. Here's the revolutionary way to knit — easy, fun, and foolproof! Beginners and experienced knitters need only master a single stitch to create their own designs with patchwork squares. More than 100 illustrations. 128pp. 6½ x 9¼.   0-486-46084-3

WUTHERING HEIGHTS, Emily Brontë. Somber tale of consuming passions and vengeance — played out amid the lonely English moors — recounts the turbulent and tempestuous love story of Cathy and Heathcliff. Poignant and compelling. 256pp. 5³⁄₁₆ x 8¼.   0-486-29256-8